RETIRE HOLISTICALLY
IN
LIFE PLAN COMMUNITIES

a.k.a.

Continuing Care Retirement Communities
(CCRCs)

How Seniors Can Successfully Select, Enter, and Thrive in a Community

Frederick Herb

Lake Union Press
Seattle, WA

Disclaimer: The information in this book and the referenced website is a best effort guide without representations and warranties as to their accuracy and completeness. The information herein is fluid, and the advice and strategies offered may not be suitable for every situation. The author and publisher are not engaged in providing legal, financial, or other professional advice. They specifically disclaim any liability that is incurred from the use and application of the contents of this book and the referenced website.

Independently Published

-

Lake Union Press
116 Fairview Ave. N., Ste. 616
Seattle, WA 98109

Quantity sales: Discounts are available on quantity purchases by life plan communities, associations, and others. Send your inquiry to admin@agingsmartly.org or the address above.

Retire Holistically in Life Plan Communities
Frederick Herb—first edition

Printed in the United States of America

How Seniors Can Successfully Select, Enter and Thrive in a Holistic Community

To my wife, Margaret, for her continued love, advice, and support while writing this book. I could not have completed it without her understanding and encouragement.

Contents

viii

List of Figures

List of Tables

Foreword

Frederick Herb has written a book that has been long needed. You, yourself, may be considering moving to a Life Plan Community, an alternative term for what was long known as a Continuing Care Retirement Community (CCRC), or you may be a child with aging parents wondering if your parents would be happier with a more communal lifestyle.

If you have any interest in the possibility of living together with others in an engaged life setting, then this is the book for you. Mr. Herb has exhaustively considered all aspects of communal life from how to start, to what questions to ask, to how to get acquainted after move-in. A decision to uproot and move into such a community is not one to be taken lightly. Frederick Herb, here, in this well-written, well-organized book provides a guide to accompany you through all the steps involved.

Speaking for myself, I share Mr. Herb's delight in his decision to move to a life plan community and to do so while still young. My wife and I did the same, Mr. Herb and his wife in Seattle, my wife and I in a beachfront community in Carlsbad, California. There are major advantages to making the move early, not least of which is the financial advantage of spreading the fixed move-in cost over a much longer period.

It's evident here that Frederick Herb has a passion for the English language. He presents complex matters with practical clarity. Moreover, Mr. Herb as a resident himself approaches his subject from the buyer's perspective in a world in which most information is sales oriented. He is not selling a product; he is explaining a choice that for many eases the transitional challenges of aging.

There is but one nationwide organization of life plan community residents, the National Continuing Care Residents Association (NaCCRA), which advocates empowerment, respect, and financial security for such residents. Mr. Herb's perspective reflects NaCCRA's core values.

It is an act of admirable responsibility, and thoughtful planning, to take the first step toward exploring the continuing care living concept. By moving to such a community while still young, vital, and engaged in the larger world, life plan community residents assure that they will not burden others and that they can provide for their own aging.

If you wish you could have a knowledgeable friend to help you to consider this attractive approach to aging, then you have found that friend here in Frederick Herb, the author of the book you now hold in your hands. Not only will he guide you in your search, he will still be here within the pages of this book to help you make the adjustment to the new world of living possibilities that awaits you.

Jack Cumming
NaCCRA Research Director

Preface

My wife, Margaret, and I moved into Mirabella Seattle seven years ago. At the time, it was a one-year-old life plan community, with 289 independent units with assisted living, memory care, and skilled nursing facilities. Having just witnessed the sudden death of Margaret's brother-in-law and our parents' end-of-life struggles several years earlier, we decided it was time for us to make the move. We decided not to burden our children with the task of finding a place for us, and we wanted to make our own decisions. We are still happy with our decision to move when we did.

Shortly after getting settled in, I joined an in-house writing workshop. Three of us were intent on writing books. Others in the group were writing family memoirs. Initially I started writing a mystery novel, but I quickly concluded that it was too competitive a genre for me to successfully publish, and my heart was not truly in it. So, I decided to write about life plan communities, having found only one published guidebook on the subject Since then there have been three more authors, but only myself and one other living in a community. As a resident author, I believe I'm able to convey the characteristics of life plan communities and the nuances for successfully selecting, entering, and adapting to community life.

My experience while living in our community includes serving as secretary on both the emergency preparedness and finance committees. My wife, Margaret, has shared with me her experiences as a council member and treasurer of both the resident association and the Mirabella Seattle Foundation, the charitable arm of Mirabella Seattle. This exposure has provided me a rich opportunity to observe the internal workings of a community.

I am also an eight year member of the National Continuing Care Residents' Association (NaCCRA). I have attended four annual conferences for LeadingAge, a six-thousand-member association for nonprofit organizations providing housing and health care for seniors. Each annual conference provides four days of morning and afternoon continuing education classes on subjects relating to life plan communities, as well as other healthcare fields. These sessions have given me a good understanding of current issues affecting seniors and their living situations.

Acknowledgments

Innumerable individuals have provided valuable information, assistance, and critique of the contents and organization of this book.

I'm particularly grateful for the support of the Mirabella writers' workshop, led by Tracy Heinlein, and its members: David Banks, Ida Curtis, Bonita Denison, Jo Roberts, Ingrid Steppic, Gisela Baxter, and Elizabeth Bret. Various resident committee members and staff within Mirabella shared information on the inner workings of the community.

As a resident in a Life Plan Community, the LeadingAge Association for nonprofit health-care organizations provided me with free admission to their annual meetings, with the opportunity to attend any of their educational sessions.

Officers and members of the National Continuing Care Residents' Association were also helpful.

Introduction

This book is intended for all seniors who are interested in their aging process and would like information on private and public health care and senior support services. It is especially for those who are relatively healthy and in their seventies and eighties, but are beginning to feel socially isolated in their current surroundings or are concerned about their care if they develop a disabling illness. The book is divided into four parts.

Following the first part on senior living, the book describes Life Plan Communities and how to select, enter, and thrive in them.

Life Plan Communities is a new brand name for Continuing Care Retirement Communities (CCRC). They are an all-inclusive category of retirement living, providing independent living and assisted, memory and nursing care as needed by their residents. The social aspect of living is emphasized.

In 2015 LeadingAge, the association for nonprofit Life Plan Communities, sponsored a survey[1] on seniors' reaction to the "Continuing Care Retirement Community" name. The finding was that the word "retirement" was a turn-off. Seniors may be retired from a full-time job, but they are not retired from life. Unlike older generations primarily seeking a safety net as they aged, the

---

[1] NameStorm Life Plan Community, http:lifeplancommunity.org .

newer generations want more choices and to be participants in their community. The new name switches the emphasis from passive care to active living and is expected to draw in residents at an earlier age.

The name change will be gradual and likely to take years for all communities to adapt. Expect the Life Plan Community name to initially be shown in the context of "Doing business as," rather than in contractual and regulatory documents.

Rebranding a Community

Today the average entry age for a resident in a Life Plan Community is the early eighties.[2] Considering the abundance of social, educational, physical, and recreational programs being offered, an appropriate average entry age is in the mid-seventies. To achieve this change, LeadingAge and many communities are changing their marketing to emphasize communal-living opportunities over health-care services via the new name Life Plan Community.

In addition to the name change, community operators are expanding their offerings to meet the desires of the emerging Boomer clientele. The Boomer generation will be seeking a social experience with a wide choice of living arrangements and contracts for service.

This book is divided into four parts.

Part One/Senior Living

This is a prelude to the remaining parts of the book, which describe life plan communities in detail. Its purpose is to encourage seniors to take charge of their journey in aging, to be aware of the hazards along the way, and to have a plan in the event of a calamity.

+ Chapter 1, "As We Age," emphasizes that seniors cannot do it alone and identifies community resources necessary to age successfully.
+ Chapter 2, "Preparations for Aging," identifies hazards along the way and resources available in times of need.

---

[2] LeadingAge 2016 Annual Meeting & Expo, session 119—The Boomer Consumer: Implications for Providers.

+ Chapter 3, "Senior-Living Landscape," identifies various programs and living arrangements available for seniors.

Part Two/Life Plan Communities

This section details what it is like to live in a life plan community.

+ Chapter 4, "Living in a Life Plan Community," describes living accommodations, amenities, and social, wellness, and continuum-of-care programs.

+ Chapter 5, "Life Plan Community Landscape," identifies the evolution, demographics, organizational types, and number of communities. Differences between nonprofit and for-profit communities are explained.

+ Chapter 6, "The Circle of Governance," describes the roles of federal, state and local government, community providers and resident organizations in governing communities.

+ Chapter 7, "Life Plan Community Finance," is a tutorial on community financing, payment plans, and contracts.

+ Chapter 8, "The Health Center," covers health services and the process for transitioning from independent living to the health-care center.

+ Chapter 9, "Is It the Right Choice?" identifies barriers to overcome in considering a community. It covers temperament, affordability issues, and impediments to moving.

Part Three/Selecting a Life Plan Community

This section covers the process for identifying and prioritizing your physical and social needs and matching them with communities being considered.

✦ Chapter 10, "Preparation for a Selection," is a guide to identify your expectations and constraints and create a list of candidates.

✦ Chapter 11, "Community Visits," covers what to consider and record during your visits and inspections.

✦ Chapter 12, "Confirming Financial Viability" is a guide on how to analyze a community's financial reports.

✦ Chapter 13, "Final Inspection," is a discussion on working with marketing and performing a final inspection on a community with a deposit

Part Four/Making the Move

Moving can be a traumatic event. This section identifies resources for accomplishing the task.

✦ Chapter 14, "Moving Arrangements," deals with staging and selling your home, financing your entrance fee, what to take, and accomplishing the move.

✦ Chapter 15, "Your New Home," covers settling in, getting into a routine, and becoming engaged in the community.

✦ Chapter 16, "Role of Family and Heirs," is about the family's involvement during crisis and at the end of life.

Appendixes

There are two appendixes at the end of the book.

+ Appendix A, "Mortality and Senior Illnesses," identifies the scary part of growing old with discussion on mortality and common disabling illnesses of the elderly.

+ Appendix B, "Resources," is a bibliography of information sources referenced in the book.

When you have read this book, you should be well equipped to do all the research necessary to make an informed decision on aging smartly and selecting appropriate living arrangement within a Life Plan Community or elsewhere.

Part One

Senior Living

In this section I identify the obstacles in aging and the means to age successfully. Support groups within communities and among health-care providers are identified. Various senior independent living and assisted-living accommodations are covered.

Chapter 1

As We Age

A range of emotions may flow over seniors as they begin their retirement years. For many it is a moment of exuberance and liberation from long commutes and the daily grind. They are now free to pursue their hobbies and explore the world. My advice to them is to pursue their dream sooner, rather than later. Others may feel that they have lost their identity, having been held in high esteem during their work years. To them I say, "Burn all your business cards and look for new endeavors, rather than clinging to the corporate fence."

Society recognizes retirement as a period of reward. Further, the steepening of the aging process may make continuing employment a burden and a hazard to oneself and others.

Most seniors plan on staying in their current home indefinitely following retirement. It is familiar, neighborly, and accessible to their routine haunts. Most likely there is no mortgage to worry about. Some seniors will downsize to a smaller home or condominium. A few will move to a senior retirement community, but still live in a single-family home environment. These are good years, with seniors typically living at home and socially engaged with old and new friends and acquaintances.

For most retirees, it is relatively easy sailing through their sixties and early seventies. There is time for travel, hobbies, sporting activities, and cultural events. While physical and mental capabilities may begin to diminish, they are still independent and in control.

The Awakening

Beginning in their late seventies, many seniors may find routine home maintenance a chore. As neighbors in their age group move on, they may begin to experience social isolation. Illnesses and injuries are more frequent, wounds heal more slowly, and there may be hearing, eyesight, and mobility issues. There is often the sense of losing independence and having to rely on others. By the eighties and nineties, the need for assisted living, memory care, or long-term nursing care is a distinct possibility.

In some cultures, the care of the elderly is established by tradition. For example, in India when seniors decide that they cannot take care of themselves, they simply pick up their pillow and move in with the oldest son. It's accepted and expected, and in return the eldest son inherits everything.

In the United States, it isn't that simple. We have a blending of cultures, geographical dispersion of families, and often a diversity of opinion among siblings as to what is best for Mom and Dad. Retirees who wish to have control of their destiny as they grow old need to be proactive and plan for their future care.

It Takes a Village

In 1996 Hillary Clinton published *It Takes a Village*. Her point was that a family alone cannot provide all the needs of their children. A child's well-being also depends on the support of individuals and groups outside of the family, that is, their community (village). Specifically, children need a nourishing environment, good schools, playgrounds, sports opportunities, and good role models.

While children emerge from being dependent to independent, elders do the opposite. As they age, they become less independent and more dependent. So, like children, they also need a caring village.

My first realization of being old was when a lady offered her seat to me on a crowded bus. My initial inclination was to decline; but I thought better of it, sat down and thanked her for her generosity. I gained a seat, and she accomplished her good deed for the day.

As seniors approach the age of seventy-five (recognized as being old), it is prudent to begin arranging for future health care and social needs. Start with an assessment of what is available in your village or community. If you are in a small community, you may find that you will have to move to have access to a full complement of anticipated services. Do consider a Life Plan Community as your village. These communities seamlessly provide all elements of health care with an abundance of social and recreational service within their self-contained campus.

Aging Blissfully

My parents were a perfect example of this. They were in good health when they retired. They stayed in their single-family home and tended to a vegetable and flower garden. They traveled, belonged to a lawn bowling club, were active at their church, and were regulars at the Elks Club.

They were members of a Health Maintenance Organization (HMO) that alluded to opening a retirement center. It never happened! Mom and Dad did not pursue other senior-living alternatives.

Except for lamenting that their friends were dying around them, life was good until my dad had a mild stroke in his mid-eighties. He refused to be treated for it and had a second stroke a few days later that landed him in the hospital and then in a nursing home for rehabilitation. His recovery was gradual, but not enough for him to return to his home, as it had many stairs at the entry. Further, I discovered that my mother had dementia and would not be able to maintain a house hold with a dependent husband.

I arranged for them to enter a light assisted-living facility. This lasted briefly until my mother started a fire by drying out Dad's pants in the oven.

I tried to convince my mother to move into a Life Plan Community, but on the tour, she was overwhelmed by the display of the health center, linen table cloths, and the sheer size of the facility. She questioned the need even though my father's health was deteriorating.

I was surprised. She was a salesperson by profession and could readily make friends, even among total strangers. I thought that she would cherish moving into a vibrant community. It was too late for them! Instead, she agreed to move into a heavy (twenty-four-hour care) assisted-living facility that served them until my father's death at age eighty-nine.

Shortly thereafter, Mom developed a bed sore from inactivity after a fall and had to be transferred to a skilled nursing facility. This facility closed a year later and Mom moved to two other nursing homes before her death at ninety-five.

The tragedy of this was that they had passed the age to successfully adapt to a community's culture, cultivate new friendships, and have an active social life. And so, it is with many seniors. As they age into their late seventies and eighties, they often fail to arrange for their future health care and social needs.

Aging Smartly

While the average life expectancy for a sixty-five-year-old is approximately eighty-four, many will barely reach seventy-five and others will live into their nineties. How are you planning your lifestyle for this period? To be on the safe side, financial planners suggest that you budget for living to ninety years or more.

Aging smartly entails having a plan where you will go for help in the event of need. As you age you need to consider changes in your physical and mental condition and assess their likely implications. Following an annual physical would be a good time to update your living plan.

Just-in-Case Planning

Health-care emergencies among the elderly often require quick placement in an assisted-living facility or nursing home. The immediate need limits the ability of the spouse or family to find the most appropriate provider.

To ensure that you will receive the best affordable care, investigate the health-care providers in your community while you're still capable of doing so. Take tours, get quotes, and ask for references in preparing your list of suitable services. When visiting a nursing home, let your senses be your guide regarding its suitability.

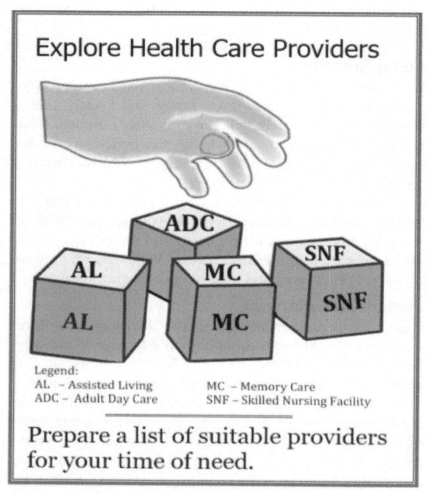

Figure 1.1. Make a list of health-care providers

Also, consider the possibility that you and your spouse may need different kinds of care, such as one needing assisted living and the other memory care. Is there a facility that provides both, so you will not be separated?

Share your preferences with your family and the person having your durable power of attorney. The best facilities may have waiting lists, so have a list of backup facilities. You may also consider getting on a wait list at your first choices. If they call and you are not yet ready, ask to be called later.

Aging Holistically

Just-in-case planning is useful in identifying and qualifying sites providing assisted living, memory care, and skilled nursing. However, it does not address the likely need of transitioning among assisted living, memory care, and skilled nursing facilities in a seamless and graceful manner. Holistic aging goes an additional step by integrating the health services seamlessly with independent-living and social functions.

Life plan communities are the dominant providers meeting an amalgamation of senior health-care needs in an independent-living setting, as well as providing a continuum of health care; the communities are the village that nurtures its residents with intellectual and wellness programs, recreation, and entertainment in a social environment.

Another holistic system on aging is currently in development in a few locations. It is continuing care at home (CCaH), which promises to provide a continuum of health-care service to seniors aging at home. What independent CCaH systems lack is the social programs that come with life plan communities.

Some life plan communities offer a CCaH program locally. The participants in their CCaH will have access to some of the sponsoring life plan community's wellness and social programs.

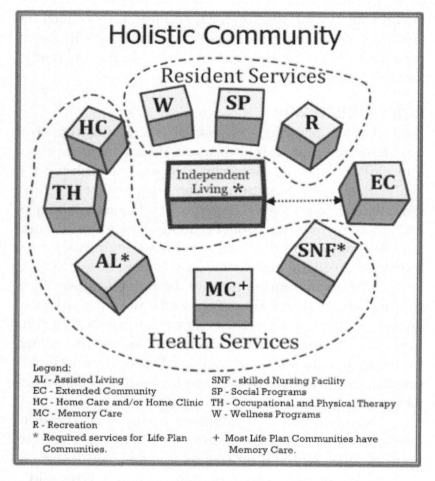

Figure 1.2. A layer of resident and health services

Summary

In this chapter, you have learned about health risks and the possibility of social isolation as seniors continue to age. I have urged seniors to plan for their future health care as they age and to be prepared should a calamity occur.

Chapter 2

Preparations for Aging

This chapter covers senior hazards and a wide set of resources for seniors in the event of calamity.

Planning for Your Care

The dilemma in senior-living arrangements is that your health-care needs may surreptitiously increase as you age, allowing you to put off planning for your future care. But since you do not know if or when an immediate need may occur, it's better to plan ahead.

While this book is about life plan communities, they are just one of many living arrangements for accommodating the elderly. The distinction is that life plan communities provide one-stop shopping, whereas other choices are more likely an interim step in a progression of accommodations, with each having more intensive health services. Whatever your current living arrangement, know where you will go if you or your spouse need greater care. If you wait until a fateful event occurs, you are likely to make poor decisions in the rush for an immediate solution. Also have a backup plan, in case your preferred accommodations are not immediately available.

Ideally, financially you should plan early in your retirement for the eventual changes that may be needed in your living arrangements. The risk in not deciding ahead is that your choices following a calamity may be very limited because of the urgency needed in planning.

Could This Happen to You?

"Mom, I got here as soon as I could," said Jerry. "The traffic on the interstate was jammed because of a truck accident earlier in the day. How is Dad, and where is he?"

"Dad is at Providence Hospital," said Grace. "He got distracted and missed the first step on the decline from Rainbow Plaza. He banged into the column at the end of the steps on his way down. Broke his right tibia, left wrist, and has a couple of fractures to his vertebrae. The doctor says that he will be in a cast for weeks and will need extensive rehab to regain his mobility...Worse , the doc warned that he may not fully recover. You know he has osteoporosis."

"That's awful...How much pain is he in? Can he see visitors? When will he be able to come home?"

"That's the problem. The hospital may release him in a couple of days, but he can't come home! He will be in a wheelchair. Our bedroom is upstairs, and there is no possibility of him navigating the stairs alone, and I don't have the strength to help him. We coul d move a bed into the living room, but there is only a half bath downstairs, and it is too small for a wheelchair. Can you and Joy take Dad in until he is back on his feet?...You have a bedroom on your first floor."

"We had a bedroom on our first floor. Joy recently convinced her boss to allow her to telecommute from home, and the bedroom is now her office. She is not going to give it up!...Besides, there are other problems. We live a hundred miles away in a small town without health-care services. How would Dad see his doctor and get rehabilitative care?"

"I'm beside myself...I don't know what to do...I was hoping that Dad could stay with you."

"Mom, the hospital has a social worker who can help us find an appropriate place while he recovers. Let's call now and schedule a meeting with the social worker. After our meeting, I will help you scout out the places being recommended for his recovery."

Where to Find Help?

This section identifies professionals and agencies that can assist if a mishap such as the one described below occurs:

The phone rang, and Jane raced to answer the call. She had been expecting one from her sister, Martha, to report on the condition of their mother, Ellen, who had been admitted to a hospital five days ago after a stroke.

"Hi, Sis. I'm at my wit's end. Just got back from the hospital. Mom is being released today and will be admitted to the Archangel Rehab Center. Dad is a mess! He was not expecting this...nor was I fo r that matter. Up until now I've not paid a lot of attention to them. They have been traveling, gardening, golfing."

"Hold on. What is a rehab center...and how long will she be there?" asked Jane.

"It is a facility that provides physical and occupational therapy to patients who have suffered a stroke or other debilitating illness. The therapy can somewhat reverse the condition or enable the patient to better cope with it."

"Are you saying that Mom may not fully recover?"

"It is unlikely...often there is only marginal improvement, and Mom's stroke was severe. It affected her speech and mobility. She may not be able to walk again."

"Oh my God, that's terrible! Can she return home?"

"Depends on how successful therapy will be and whether Dad will be up to handling all of her daily needs...Dad has not cooked a meal in his lifeHe doesn't strike me as being the caregiver type... but maybe he is adaptable. However, their home cannot accommodate a wheelchair without major renovation."

"How long will they keep her in the rehab center, and who pays for it?"

"Rehab is paid for by Medicare until they determine that there is no further improvement in her condition. It could be days or weeks, but there is a one-hundred-day limit. In the meantime we need to help Dad in planning for her continuing care. The social worker at the hospital advised him not to plan on taking it on alone; he could end up in the hospital too."

"Martha, can you take her in?"

"I dearly love Mom and Dad, but that is not a burden that I would put my family through. We do not have a spare bedroom. A teenage boy and girl are enough of a handful. Our house is not wheelchair accessible either. Are you offering?"

"I'm across the country and often travel for my job. However, I have some slack time now and will come out and help you and Dad decide what to do. I can be there in a couple of day s. I'll let Dad know that I'll be staying with him."

"Great. Dad and I will appreciate your help."

Commentary.

Like Martha, Jane, and their parents, most people are unprepared when calamity occurs. They are likely unaware of the process for obtaining home-care providers or placement in suitable health-care facilities, such as adult home care, assisted living, memory care, or skilled nursing. The need is often unexpected. It can be a time of shock and awe, demanding immediate attention.

Following are planning guides for your well-being and a list of sources and services available to seniors and their families in time of need. They include referral ser-vices and placement agencies. While most are profes-sional and have the client's interest foremost in mind, some are not. I identify how to differentiate between those that arrange suitable placement versus those that take advantage of the time constraints and find a "bed for a head" at the location that pays the highest finder's fee.

Things to Consider

Your retirement planning should contemplate the following:

+ **Fall Prevention.** Falls are the leading cause of emergency room visits among seniors. My mother always preached not to walk with my hands in my pockets. I ignored her then, but now I follow that practice. Free hands assist in regaining balance should you trip and protecting your head should you fall. My other habits are to look down with every third step while walking to avoid a surprise and to use the handrail when going down a set of stairs. Gyms and wellness centers have exercise equipment for improving one's balance and strengthening muscles and bones.

    As an aside, be aware that you should not pull up a fallen person, since pulling may cause further damage. Rather, provide a chair or prop so the fallen person can get up alone, or wait for medical personnel to arrive.

+ *Health Care.* Look for preventative health-care services providing health education, community-based health screening, and counseling about prescription-drug programs. Be aware of what is available for short- and long-term health care in your community. Elders as well as youths need good nutrition to be healthy. Are you able to routinely prepare nutritionally balanced meals or have routine access to nutritional meals? A third of US communities are deficient in this area.

+ **Senior Services.** Short-term care for recoverable injury and illnesses is covered by traditional health insurance, Medicare, Medicare Advantage, and HMO programs. None of these programs cover long-term health care, however.

Long-Term Care Insurance. Long-term care policies comprovide a specific per month dollar amount, generally with a growth/inflation adjustment, to help cover the beneficiary's cost for assisted living, memory care, or nursing care. Typically policyholders qualify for benefits when they need substantial assistance with two or more activities of daily living (ADL), as well as support for severe cognitive impairment. ADLs include such things as eating, bathing, dressing, toileting, and so on. Policies may require certification of need from a doctor or specialist and have a wait period before payment begins.

The ideal time to acquire long-term care insurance is before or shortly after retirement. Otherwise, you may not be eligible, or the cost could be prohibitive. There are a lot of choices in these policies, so review and compare carefully. Also, verify that the health providers you have in mind qualify for the insurance coverage.

✦ **Exercise and Wellness.** Exercise is vital to maintaining alertness and muscle tone. Do you have access to fitness programs for older adults? Again, a third of US communities do not.

✦ **Social Outlets.** Are there senior centers within walking distance or a short drive? Do they offer activities and events that suit your interests?

✦ **Frendship.** Can you cultivate new friends as your previous friends move away or pass on? If not, isolation may affect your well-being. Family and friends may not notice because of their busy lives. Isolation is insidious because it advances slowly without much notice. Senior centers and retirement communities can help in filling the void.

✦ **Transportation.** Does your community provide for the mobility needs of an aging population, such as wheelchair lifts on all buses and door-to-door transportation services for the handicapped?

✦ **Public Safety/Emergency Services**. Are there emergency medical services nearby? Can they be reached within minutes? Is the program well-funded, with fully trained medics? Are there community programs for abused and neglected elders?

Hospital Social Workers

Should you or your loved one end up in a hospital, at the time of discharge, the staff will provide physician orders and coordinate the handoff and transportation to the designated care provider.

In the event of a major disability, the hospital social worker may provide a list of agencies and providers that could include medical device suppliers, home-care providers, caregivers, psychological support groups, adult day-care facilities, Meals on Wheels, physical and occupational therapists, and so on. Hospital social workers will provide an idea of the long-term outlook and advise on how to look for long-term-care living facilities. They are a critical resource in time of need.

Gerontology Case Managers

These are licensed and accredited professionals with special skills in geriatrics and members of the Aging Life Care Association, formerly the National Association of Professional Geriatric Case Managers (NAPGCM). They are either nurses or social workers who have taken advanced courses in geriatrics and have received certification or accreditation from one of the following organizations:

+ **Nursing track certification** is provided by the National Academy of Certified Care Managers (NACCM)[3] with the title Care Manager Certified (CMC) or by the Commission for Case Manager Certification (CCMC)[4] with the title certified case manager (CCM).

+ **Social Worker certification** is provided by the National Association of Social Workers (NASW)[5] with the title certified advanced social work case manager (C-ASWCM) or certified social work case manager (C-SWCM).

Gerontology case managers (GCMs) are concierge-care advisers. Their purpose is to help seniors maintain their independence as they grow older, plan health-maintenance programs as needed, and refer their clients to appropriate clinical physicians and therapists. They are important advisers whom elders and their family

---

[3] National Academy of Certified Care Managers, http://www.naccm.net/.

[4] Commission for Case Manager Certification, https://ccmcertification.org .

[5] National Association of Social Workers (NASW), http://www.naswdc.org/.

members should call upon when an elder begins to need care or assistance. Services that they can provide include:

+ **Analyzing** clients' care needs and identifying resources to enable them to stay in their homes and maintain independence.

+ **Identifying** appropriate senior-living alternatives that are in the best interest of the client.

+ **Assisting** the client and family in selecting a nursing home for a short or long-term stay.

+ **Acting** as an advocate on behalf of the family members who cannot assist the patient because of time or distance limitations or lack of knowledge.

The task of finding and engaging caregivers can be overwhelming. Case managers are a wonderful resource in a crisis as well as in a routine situation. Like other medical professionals, geriatric case managers charge a fee for service. Depending on their involvement, it may be at an hourly or monthly rate. You can find a certified GCM from the Aging Life Care Association's directory.[6]

Ask to see a copy of credentials before you engage a GCM, particularly if you find someone you like from an Internet search. There is a possibility that such individuals are neither licensed nor certified.

As a guardian, I was very satisfied with the arrangements that a care manager made for the placement of my cousin with Alzheimer's disease.

---

[6] Find an Aging Life Care Expert,

http://memberfinder.caremanager.org/index.php/ff/advancedSearch#results .

Elder-Care Placement Agencies

These agencies help seniors and their families find placement in appropriate health-care facilities such as adult home care, assisted living, memory care, or skilled nursing for short or long terms as the situation dictates. The process starts by gathering information on the client's medical and social needs, location preferences, and financial capability as private pay or for state assistance. They then determine the appropriate facilities having vacancies. They will provide a list of referrals for the client to visit. They may offer to accompany the client on his or her visits.

If the client selects a recommended referral, and the client and provider agree on the level and cost of the service, the transaction with the referral/placement agency is complete. Some agencies may make post-move-in visits to ensure that the client is satisfied and is appropriately cared for.

Warning

It sounds simple, but there is a catch with placement and referral agencies. With the advent of the Internet, these agencies have become a growth industry, with inexpensive marketing through web servers. Some firms will advertise under two or more names with distinctively different web page designs. More importantly, they have changed their business model from one that bills the client for service, to collecting a finder's fee from the provider. They advertise free service as a lure. Even those in the business, who prefer the old way, cannot compete, because almost all others advertise their service as free.

In business, fiduciary responsibility is to the party that pays. Placement and referral agencies are analogous to the real-estate brokerage business, where the seller pays. The buyer must look out for himself or herself. However, there is a difference: real-estate brokers and their salespeople are licensed and regulated.

You must understand that the placement agencies are financially motivated to make referrals based on their agreements with providers. The placement fee will typically be one-half to the full amount of the provider's first-month fee. Consequently, referral agency customers need to do their homework in selecting an agency.

Consider recommendations or referrals from those that you trust. Before using a placement-referral agency, ask about the qualifications of its staff. What is their educational background and years of experience in the field? Do they have any licensed nurses or social workers, and are any accredited by the NAPGCM? Talk to the person who will specifically be working with you. If you become uncomfortable, walk away. There is no charge unless you have agreed to pay a fee for service.

That said, there are competent agencies that are advocates for their clients. The trick is finding them. Candidates should have a strong staff, provide full disclosure of their process, and have a code of ethics.

Regulation and Licensing

Unlike geriatric case managers, senior referral and placement agencies are neither licensed nor regulated. States license child and job referral and placement agencies, but not those servicing seniors. There is one exception: Washington State began doing so in 2010. Arizona did from 2002 to 2005, but is no longer doing so.

Oregon has a membership-based association named Oregon Senior Referral Agency Association (OSRAA)[7]. It requires members to abide by a code of ethics that is on its web site as well as a member search engine.

Washington State's legislation is titled "Elder and Vulnerable Adult Referral Agency Act," that is described in the Revised Code or Washington (RCW), chapter 18.330.[8] RCW.

In the absence of regulation, users of these services need to be diligent and thoroughly check them out before engaging their service. Be wary of signing any documents with a provider until you are satisfied with their competency and ability to service your needs.

Summary

This chapter identifies the perils of aging and steps that can be taken to diminish the risk and how to find suitable help in the event of a problem. You learn about the breadth and depth of service offerings by health-care professionals and a guide on identifying those who truly serve your interest.

---

[7]Oregon Senior Referral Agency Association, http://osraa.com/.

[8] Washington RCW, chapter
http://app.leg.wa.gov/rcw/default.aspx?cite=18.330 .

Chapter 3

Senior Living Landscape

Following retirement, most seniors continue living independently in a single or multifamily home. A decade or so later, they are confronted with the possibility of needing health-care assistance. There are a number of alternatives to consider, depending upon their likely health-care needs and financial ability.

Senior Services

"The Maturing of America II"[9] 2010 survey of fourteen hundred local governments identifies their ability to meet the needs of their aging constituents. The survey was sponsored by MetLife and National Association of Area Agencies on Aging (n4a) and conducted by the International City/County Management Association ICMA. The survey found that the preparedness of local government varies by population density and area.

New England and Pacific Coast regions consistently show higher percentages of available services than other areas of the country. Likewise, urban areas provided many more services than rural areas. Excerpts from the survey follow:

---

[9] The Maturing of America—Communities Moving Forward for an Aging Population, June 2011, https://www.metlife.com/assets/cao/foundation/MaturingOfAmerica_FINAL_Rpt.pdf .

✦ **Health Services**. Over two-thirds (69 percent) of local governments report the availability of health-care services that meet a range of needs. However, communities with larger populations are far more likely to provide or deliver these (all local governments of one million plus report doing so); older adults in more rural areas are at a significant disadvantage in securing health-care services. This disparity is also true of prescription-drug programs (other than Medicare Part D), wellness programs, preventive screenings, and immunizations

✦ **Nutrition.** Respondents indicate that home-delivered meals programs are available in 85 percent of communities, and more than half of local governments report that the meal provider or deliverer is a nonprofit or faith-based organization. A high percentage of communities (73 percent) also report the availability of nutrition education programs.

✦ **Exercise and Wellness**. Over 70 percent of communities report the availability of exercise classes tailored to specific health concerns, such as heart disease, arthritis, diabetes and falls, and nearly 90 percent report the availability of local parks and other venues that have safe, easy-to-reach walking/biking trails. The Pacific Coast region leads the nation in the availability of both initiatives.

✦ **Transportation.** Fifty-six percent of the communities provide "dial a ride" or door-to-door transportation services, either free or at a modest cost. Forty percent of the communities reported having road signage that meets the needs of older drivers.

+ **Public Safety/Emergency Services.** Two-thirds of US communities have a system to locate older adults who become ill or wander due to Alzheimer's or other forms of dementia. Thirty percent have prevention programs for elder abuse and neglect.

+ **Affordable Housing.** While most housing rents are at market rate, a significant amount is available for less through annuities, charitable giving and government subsidies, such as Section 8 and property tax relief for doing so. For example, a listing of providers for a thousand nonprofit housing and healthcare communities with 68,086 affordable living units is contained in the 2016 LeadingAge Ziegler 150 report.[10] Once on the website do a find for affordable.

+ **Housing Modification.** Half of the communities reported having home modification programs to help older adults modify existing homes to accommodate physical limitations.

+ **Taxation/Finance**. Two-thirds of communities provide tax relief for older adults living on limited incomes.

Community Support Organizations

There are a significant number of local government and nonprofit organizations that help seniors remain independent. However, there is no national unifying

---

[10] "Tables 4-15a, 6.2 & 6.3, LZ 150 Providers of Affordable Housing", 2016 LeadingAge Ziegler 150, https://www.ziegler.com/z-media/3215/2016-leadingage-ziegler-150-publication_final.pdf .

organization; so there is not a common name, and the breadth and depth of the programs and services vary greatly among communities.

Programs and services that may be provided include social programs, Medicare and health insurance consulting, senior outreach, caregiver services, and home service. Home services may include minor home repair and yard maintenance, housekeeping, grocery shopping, and transportation. Most of the provided services are dependent upon volunteers.

The best way to find providers in your locality is to Google "senior neighborhood community program services in your location."

Villages

Villages in this context are nonprofit 501(c)(3) grassroots organizations consisting of neighborhood seniors who aspire to stay in their homes and develop a local community to enrich their lives while aging. Villages are intended to address the unmet needs of older adults as they age. Services typically include health, wellness, social and educational programs, home repair, transportation, and other needs, so members can remain at home as long as possible. The villages operate with volunteers and a paid staff. Revenue comes from member dues, donations, and in some cases, community or government grants.

Villages are a rather new approach for senior support. The oldest villages date to 2002 or thereabouts. At last count, there were 237 active villages and 93 villages in development. Over 80 percent are members of the Village to Village Network. Total membership for all villages is approximately thirty thousand with an average per village of one hundred fifty members. While this count may seem large, it is a pittance in comparison to the number of seniors aging at home. Most villages are located along the north Atlantic Coast and the Pacific Coast areas.

The national organization, Village to Village (VtV) Network,[11] had its tenth annual gathering in 2018. The VtV Network provides support and resources to established as well as start-up villages. For more information, a map of the villages, and a tool for searching by location or name, go to their website shown in the footnote.

Synergy among Villages and Life Plan Communities

While villages have a common goal of assisting seniors in aging at home, there are limits as to what they can accomplish individually. Unlike most senior-living providers that are well-established, villages are young organizations, diverse in their size, structure, and ability. They are protective of their autonomous grassroots and member-driven culture. Yet they recognize the need to establish relationships with other providers, be it in the form of a sponsor, partnership, affiliation, or alliance.

Many life plan communities have a strategic relationship with their neighboring villages and offer use of their extensive facilities, services, and programs to village members as a goodwill gesture and an enticement for new residents. Over 50 percent of the largest non-profit life plan communities offer some home- and community-based services to nonresidents in their community.

---

[11] Village to villagyphwnatione network, http://www.vtvnetwork.org .

Remaining at Home

As I begin this section, I'm reminded of a newspaper cartoon by Hilary Price. It shows two elderly gentlemen sitting on a park bench. The older one, holding a cane, says that his son sat him down and said, "Pops...we need to talk about aging in place." The younger gentleman looks at him in a puzzled manner without saying a word. The older gentleman continues with "Aging in place of what?"

The cartoon illustrates that many seniors are oblivious to the possibility of not being able to continue living at home. For most seniors, remaining at home is their preferred choice upon retiring. It has the obvious advantages of retaining their current support group and nearby friends and avoiding the need to relocate. However, as seniors age, the advantages of living at home begin to fade.

Most seniors will age at home until they are no longer able to do so. Some will extend the time they can successfully age at home by modifying the house to Americans with Disabilities Act (ADA) standards so it is wheelchair and walker compliant inside and outside.

Often when a spouse becomes dependent, the able-bodied spouse will attempt to be the sole care provider. It works while the care is light or infrequent; but heavy or continual care needs will result in anxiety, burn-out or illness of the sole care provider. The caring spouse needs to know when to call it quits and make other arrangements before it becomes an intolerable hardship.

So often, those aging at home do not plan for the eventuality that they will need outside care and if the need occurs suddenly, their chances of suitable placement quickly diminishes.

Wealthy couples can often live at home success-fully with a live-in aide or nurse, augmented with ar-rangements for part-time help as needed. It is not cheap and requires skill or professional help in vetting the health-care applicants.

Preparing to Age at Home

A research study, "Aging in Place in America",[12] commissioned by Clarity and The EAR Foundation, that examines the attitudes and anxieties of the nation's elderly population, show that the clear majority of seniors (89 percent) want to age in place or grow older without having to move from their homes. Yet more than half are concerned about their ability to do so. Their primary concerns are:

+ **health problems** (53 percent);

+ **memory problems** (26 percent); and

+ **inability to drive or get around** (23 percent).

As seniors' physical and mental capabilities grad-ually diminish, they should periodically adjust their rou-tine, such as arranging for housekeeping and yard service.

Further, seniors' houses should be modified soon enough to accommodate mobility problems following an illness or a fall. Mobility aids, such as crutches, walkers, and wheelchairs, require flat entries or ramps, wide doors and hallways, enlarged bathrooms, low counters, and consolidation of the living area to the ground floor. Basically, living spaces need to be brought up to ADA standards to accommodate seniors' mobility problems.

---

[12] Prince Market Research, "Clarity Final Report: Aging in America", August 20, 2007, https://www.slideshare.net/clarityproducts/clarity-2007-aginig-in-place-in-america-2836029 .

Diminished vision, dementia, and reflex problems put seniors at risk while driving cars. On a per mile basis, seniors have the highest driving accident rate. Seniors, particularly those outside of urban areas, need to plan for alternative transportation when the day arrives when they are no longer able to drive themselves.

Questions seniors need to ask themselves about continuing to live at home include: Should the need arise, will their spouse, family, or friends be willing and able to help them with the basic activities of daily living, such as feeding, bathing, dressing, and grooming? At what point will there be a need for a part-time or full-time in-home care provider? In a worst-case scenario, is there room for a live-in care provider?

Long-term in-home around-the-clock skilled nursing care is out of reach for all except the wealthiest. Not to be overlooked is the difficulty of finding and retaining competent care providers when needed.

Cost to Remodel to ADA Standards

Should you decide to age at home, it would be prudent to modify your home to ADA standards prior to an unexpected need. Like insurance, it is better to have it and not need it than not have access to your home should the need arise.

The cost to bring a home to ADA standards varies greatly depending on its size and layout. The following are national average cost for disability modifications from Fixr.com,[13] that provides cost guides for home remodeling projects.

---

[13] Fixr, Inc., Disability Modeling Cost, May 2017, https://www.fixr.com/cost-Guides.html#group_b07be56f0d7282ab73b04ebc7f4a48e0 .

+ **Bathroom.** A bathroom will require extensive modification, such as providing a barrier-free entry to the shower stall, additional grab bars, nonslip flooring, a higher toilet, and vanity modification so a wheelchair can slide beneath. The room needs to be spacious enough so an occupant in a wheelchair can rotate 360 degrees, that may require moving a wall or increasing the door width. The national average cost is $9,000.

+ **Kitchen.** In the event that a handicapped person will be using the kitchen, the cabinets, counters and appliances will have to be rearranged so the occupant has easy access without stretching or standing. Typical costs will be $15,000 to $20,000 for a complete kitchen remodel.

+ **Ramps and Handrails.** Steps both in and out of the home must be replaced with a ramp and handrail. Assume $2000 for an outside ramp and $400 for each inside ramp. A chairlift to another floor will add $3,000 to $4,000.

Moving in with Family

Often a child or children will encourage their elderly parent(s) to move in with them. For many this may be the only financially viable solution, short of Medicaid. The interpersonal relationship among seniors and other household members will have a large bearing on the success of this transition. Further, the family must consider the cost to upgrade the dwelling to ADA standards if necessary.

Retirement Communities

These communities, intended for empty nesters, became popular in the 1960s, following Del Webb's huge development of Sun City near Phoenix, Arizona. His theme was sun and fun, with friendship, socialization, and recreation. He has successfully delivered on the promise, while there has been mixed success among other developers.

These communities may consist of single-family homes, cottages, apartments, or condominiums that are consistent with local surroundings. Living unit occupancy, as determined by the operator, may be by purchase, lease, or rental. Roughly, there are quarter million units in the United States.

The operators provide services such as home maintenance, housekeeping, dining, transportation, and social and wellness programs. Amenities may include spas, beauty salons, a clubhouse, pools, tennis courts, and access to golf courses for social and physical stimulation.

Those considering buying in to a community should verify that the common facilities and amenities are currently operational and adequately funded before purchasing.

Adult Family Care Homes

Adult family care homes (AFCHs) are also referred to as adult family homes or adult family home care, and there are thousands of them throughout the United States. They are licensed by the states, with a registered nurse periodically visiting each home. AFCHs are like boardinghouses in that they are in a private residence, licensed to provide housing, meals, and personal-care services to older people and disabled adults who are unable to live independently. The care may be short or long term. AFCHs are owned and operated by licensed providers, who usually live with the residents they serve.

AFCHs typically house four to six residents. Socialization is generally limited to those in residence. If resident quarters and common areas are cramped, a disruptive or noisy resident can make life miserable for all.

Services include observation, assistance with activities of daily living, and dispensing of medications to elders and disabled adults as required. Typically, the provider is a registered or practical nurse, with an aide to assist or as backup.

AFCHs are intended to be a less costly alternative for individuals who do not need twenty-four-hour nursing supervision. The cost will vary depending on the location, ambiance, amenities, accommodations, and individual services. Generally, costs average 50 to 75 percent of that of nursing homes. Some residents may qualify for Medicaid or veterans' benefits to offset the cost.

Assisted-Living Facilities

According to the National Center for Assisted Living (NCAL), there are over thirty thousand assisted-living communities nationwide that serve one million seniors.[14] The communities provide long-term care for individuals requiring assistance with basic daily activities such as bathing, dressing, toileting, and mobility. These services are referred to as custodial care. Assisted living is

---

[14] NCAL, "Number and Size of Communities," April 28, 2007, https://www.ahcancal.org/ncal/facts/Pages/Communities.aspx .

regulated by the states, and some will allow services to include medication assistance and reminders. The median age for residents is eighty-five.

The availability and coverage of a nurse and aides can vary greatly among assisted-living facilities, so prospective residents should inquire what the staff coverage is throughout the day. Is a nurse on call or on-site? Will the coverage meet your anticipated needs?

Assisted living allows residents the dignity and respect of their independence in a social setting with minor medical support. It is often provided in a residential setting, with each unit typically being a one-bedroom or studio apartment without a kitchen, since all meals are provided in a common dining area. Some may offer kitchenettes and two bedrooms for couples. There are common rooms for socialization and dining. Entertainment and scheduled transportation for shopping and medical appointments are often provided.

Some assisted-living providers combine dementia patients with their assisted-living patients if there are not enough dementia patients to warrant a separate facility. This puts an additional burden on their staff, who must intervene when conflicts occur between the two types of patients. Alzheimer's patients may become agitated and possibly hostile if not approached in a caring manner.

Although many federal laws impact assisted living, the licensing of assisted-living facilities is at the state level. More than two-thirds of the states use the licensure term "assisted living" or a similar term. The second most used term is "residential care." Other licensure terms include boarding house, basic care facility, community residence, enriched housing program, home for the aged, personal-care home, and shared housing establishment.

All states regulate assisted-living facilities to a greater or lesser degree. There is no universal standard among the states. While rules may vary from state to state, they will include such things as a minimum staff-to-resident ratio and the number of licensed personnel throughout the day. States also have an interest in the efficacy and efficiency of services since they pay most of the cost for Medicaid residents.

The specific regulations and statement of services for each state can be found in two referenced documents from the National Center for Assisted Living (NCAL) Assisted Living[15] and the US Department of Health and Human Services[16]. Collectively, these documents average 14 pages of information per state, although there is a wide disparity on page count among states. The information includes licensure term, regulatory definitions, scope of care, move-in/move-out requirements, resident

---

[15]"Assisted Living State Regulatory Review 2013", Karl Polzer, National Center for Assisted Living, March 2013, https://www.ahcancal.org/ncal/advocacy/regs/Documents/2013_reg_review.pdf .

[16] "Compendium of Residential Care and Assisted Living Regulations and Policy": 2015 Edition, Paula Carder, Janet O'Keeffe and Christine O'Keeffe, RTI International, Office of The Assistant Secretary for Planning and Evaluation (ASPE), 06/15/15, https://aspe.hhs.gov/basic-report/compendium-residential-care-and-assisted-living-regulations-and-policy-2015-edition .

assessment, medication management, physical plant requirements, residents allowed per room, staffing requirement, training and certification, regulatory terms and definitions, food service and dietary provisions, provisions for dementia, background checks, and inspection and monitoring requirements.

Memory-Care Facilities

The care of dementia and Alzheimer's patients requires a specialized facility and skills exceeding basic custodial care. Memory care is the socially preferred term for the care of these patients. A list of all the illnesses contributing to dementia can be found in Appendix A, "Mortality and Senior Illnesses."

State regulation of memory-care facilities is included in the regulations for assisted living and other forms of community living.

The facility needs to be quiet, friendly, and with familiar surroundings, such as visual reminders of the resident's past. The prerequisite staff's skills are more social than medical. In addition to providing custodial care, the staff needs to know how to engage the residents without startling them and how to lead them in group activities, such as sing-alongs and certain games.

The other element of memory care is effective security so the patients cannot wander off. I have a personal story regarding this. I was guardian for a cousin in the 1980s with Alzheimer's who wandered one winter evening from his care center, causing a lot of anxiety and concern. He was not found until the next morning. Fortunately, he was OK. At the time, it was against the law to lock patients in. While dementia patients may discover the way out, they rarely find their way back.

There are stand-alone memory-care facilities as well as ones contained within assisted living and life plan communities.

Nursing Facilities

According to a Centers for the Medicare & Medicaid Services' report,[17] "there were 15,640 nursing facilities nationwide in 2014, serving 1.4 million residents at any given time." The demand peak was in 2005 and has been receding slightly since then, probably because improvements in health services and medication have reduced the need for skilled medical care. Most nursing facilities stand alone. The remainder are associated with life plan communities, hospitals, and assisted-living facilities.

Nursing homes provide custodial as well as skilled nursing care. Skilled nursing needs are usually short-term and for senior mostly covered by Medicare. Custodial nursing care is private pay or covered by Medicaid for seniors who qualify. However, if custodial services are included in a skilled service written plan of care, they, as well as the associated skilled service, will be covered by Medicare.

---

[17] Nursing Home Data Compendium 2015 Edition, Figure 1.1. Number of Nursing Homes: United States, 2005–2014 and Figure 1.5. Number of Certified Nursing Home Beds, by Occupancy: United States, 2005–2014, https://www.cms.gov/Medicare/Provider-Enrollment-and-Certification/CertificationandComplianc/Downloads/nursinghomedata-compendium_508-2015.pdf .

Available Treatments

There are twelve or more conditions that a skilled nursing center may routinely be called upon to manage. Most providers will provide the common ones, but may not provide specialized procedures that are in low demand.

Table 3.1. Skilled nursing procedures [18]

Common Nursing Procedures	
Cardiac Care	Central Line
Diabetes Management	Enteric Nutrition
IV Therapy	Orthopedic Care
Pain Management	PICC Line
Postsurgical Care	Stroke Rehabilitation
Tracheotomy Care	Wound Care
Specialized Nursing Procedures	
Active Drug and Alcohol Dependencies	Acute Psychiatric Episodes
IV Chemotherapy On-Site	On-Site Dialysis
Ventilator Care	Others

Skilled Nursing Inspections

States regulate nursing facilities, and Medicare certifies them for senior care under Medicare Part A. Both federal and state personnel conduct annual and spot inspections of nursing facilities.

The Centers for Medicare & Medicaid Services (CMS) is responsible for monitoring the care of all beneficiaries of Medicaid and Medicare. Regarding skilled nursing facilities (SNFs), CMS contracts out this responsibility to the states and then monitors their performance. The CMS monitoring program is the Federal Oversight/Support Survey (FOSS). Elements of FOSS include the following:

---

[18] Consensus with interviews.

✦ Accompanying state inspectors on annual surveys within nine- to fifteen-month intervals

✦ Performing a comparative survey a month or less later than the state's survey

✦ Annual state performance evaluation of survey frequency, quality, appropriateness, and effectiveness of enforcement

CMS Five-Star Rating System

The Centers for Medicare & Medicaid Services (CMS) has a five-star quality rating system to help consumers, their families, and caregivers compare nursing homes more easily and to help identify areas about which you may want to ask questions. The three components of the rating system are:

✦ **State Health Inspections** on the scope, and severity of deficiencies identified during the last three annual inspections.

✦ **Staffing Rating** based on the levels of registered nurse hours per resident day and total hours for registered nurses, licensed practical nurses, and nurse aides per resident day. The staffing measures are case-mix-adjusted for different levels of resident-care needs across nursing homes.

✦ **Quality Measures Rating** based on performance of eighteen quality measures (QMs) for eight long stays and three short stays.

The results of the inspections and ratings are available from a database at

Data.Medicare.Gov.[19].

The rating database can be downloaded either as a Microsoft Access file or comma-separated values (CSV) file. The database consists of tables, with the nursing facilities arranged in rows and their attributes and scores in columns.

Currently, there are 15,560 licensed and certified nursing facilities. The primary table, "Providerinfo,"[20] has seventy-nine columns, providing a staggering amount of information. For laypeople, the attributes of most interest are name, location, phone number, legal entity (LBN), ownership, bed count (BED-CERT), CCRC (Y or N), overall rating, survey rating, quality rating, incidents, and complaints. In addition, there are tables for deficiencies and penalties.

Overall Rating: The overall five-star rating is a composite of the health inspection, staffing, and QM ratings identified above. It is essentially a one number report card on the performance of a nursing facility. Instructions on how to obtain the rating for a nursing facility is covered in chapter 11 under, Skilled Nursing Issues.

---

[19] Data.Medicare.Gov, "Table Providerinfo_January2016, Columns B as name & W, as overall rating, https://data.medicare.gov/data/archives/nursing-home-compare .

Continuing Care at Home

Continuing care at home (CCaH) is a rather new concept started by a few life plan communities that decided to extend their reach to provide at-home health services to nearby residential clients. This service is made possible with advances in medical diagnostics allowing medical personnel to monitor a patient's condition remotely, thus diminishing the presence of skilled personnel on-site.

Separately, there is an abundance of agencies that provide caregivers offering custodial care at home to assist with daily activities either on a part-time or full-time basis. The cost is generally manageable because skilled medical personnel are not routinely needed to provide help with daily living activities.

A few Life Plan Communities allow CCcaH participants to use their community's wellness facilities and attend some social events as a good jester and marketing ploy. These communities are mostly in the northeastern part of the United States. However, their numbers are growing.

Summary

In this chapter, you have heard about community and government services that are available to seniors. There is information on upgrading your house to ADA standards and the possibility of obtaining health-care services at home. You have read about the various offerings of independent and assisted-living accommodations as well as how to obtain the quality rating of nursing facilities.

Part Two

Life Plan Communities

Life Plan Communities is a brand (doing business as) term for senior housing with independent living and a continuum of health care until end of life. In a legal and regulatory sense, they are licensed as Continuing Care Retirement Communities. Most communities have not yet adopted the new name. The name change is being sponsored by LeadingAge, the nonprofit industry's association[21]. The name along with expanded active living offerings is intended to attract the Baby Boomer generation. In writing this book, I've taken risk on being too early in using this term.

This section of six chapters is devoted to describing Life Plan Communities. It describes the living accommodations, resident benefits, and services. There is narration on living within a community. Opportunities for resident participation in a community are covered.

The evolution of the communities, their current organizational structure, geographic differences in size; the role of local, state, federal, and internal governance is explained. Finance issues and payment plans are covered. Each of the components of the health center is described as well as the process of transferring from independent living to the health center. Lastly, there is

---

[21] Life Plan Community Organization
http://lifeplancommunity.org

discussion on assimilating into a community, and personality traits that may not be suitable for living within a community.

Chapter 4

Living in a Life Plan Community

Most people entering life plan communities will be young enough to actively participate in their communities. Amenities and activities are what keep residents satisfied. They may be retired from working for a living, but they are not retired from being engaged and living their senior lives to the fullest. Unlike most of those entering other senior living facilities, only a few life-plan community residents enter with the notion of "just take care of me." They are movers and shakers determined to be participants in their daily living experience.

Living Accommodations

Most people enter a community as independent-living residents. It is senior living and typically limited to age sixty and above. Independent housing typically consists of apartments, townhouses, or cottages, depending upon the physical setting. Accommodations and spaciousness will vary depending on the residential setting, the facility's age, and the targeted income level. Newer or recently refurnished life plan communities will generally be more spacious than their older brethren. Their kitchens will be larger and well equipped, floor plans will be open, and a washer and a dryer will be in the unit. Spaciousness and accommodations may compare with condominiums of the same vintage.

Most life plan communities require prospective residents to be in relatively good health when they move into an independent living unit. Communities, however, cannot discriminate against prospective residents who are wheelchair-bound if they can demonstrate that they can manage for themselves and live independently. Buildings built or renovated following passage of the Americans with Disabilities Act (ADA)[22] will have some of their independent living units ADA-compliant, with bathrooms, bedrooms, and hallways capable of accommodating a wheelchair.

Assisted-living and memory-care units will be studios or one-bedroom units without a kitchen since all meals are provided. There may be two-bedroom units for couples.

Nursing accommodations will be in rooms for one or two occupants. Most new or recently renovated communities will be equipped and furnished primarily for a single occupant who is a contract resident. There may be a few lower cost double-occupant rooms for private pay or Medicaid nonresident patients.

Community's Carefree Benefits

The benefits of living in a life plan community include the following:

+ The ability to come and go as you choose
+ Participation in social programs, outings, and activities sponsored by the community
+ The ability to take advantage of wellness programs, including a fitness center and perhaps a pool
+ Shedding house maintenance and repair concerns and enjoying housekeeping services

---

[22] Americans with Disabilities Act was passed in 1990, https://www.ac-cess-board.gov/the-board/laws/americans-with-disabilities-act-intro .

✦ The peace of mind in knowing that your future health-care needs will be taken care of

✦ A community support system that's there for you in your time of need

✦ Opportunities to give back to the extended community as a volunteer

✦ Dining and meal options that are tailored to senior needs

✦ Transportation for shopping, errands, church, and local events, thus eliminating or diminishing the need for a car

✦ Personal and physical security while on the premises.

Community Services

The functions and services provided within a Life Plan Community follows:

Figure 4.1. Life Plan Community Services

Resident Services:

+ Reception or concierge services, such as arranging trips and transportation, providing valet service if applicable, and assisting resident committees and clubs in their endeavors

+ Distribution of information on activities, events, outings, and administration announcements; and facilitation of communications among residents and staff

+ Monitoring the status of declining residents who may soon need assistance, and alerting their families to these observations and coordinating future support with them

✦ General security within the complex and 24/7 security within the health center. Security personnel are the first responders when a resident trips a Vigil alarm, a wireless, wearable device to signal for help.

✦ Provision for a hair salon.

Dining Services

Dining services is the most labor-intensive activity in a community, with a significant number of kitchen personnel and wait staff. Many independent residents have their main meal in the dining room. There are often two seatings for dinner, and reservations may be required for large groups. Many residents will have an additional meal or two throughout the day in the cafe, bistro, or dining room.

Variety is important. A typical offering may be a choice of starter plates, entrees, and dessert from a weekly or monthly menu, with a daily special or two. Many communities also have a buffet for those looking for something other than what is on the à la carte menu, and some residents want takeout or a quick meal. The kitchen will need to accommodate common dietary restrictions, such as gluten-free diet, and to withhold ingredients upon request, such as bell peppers. Catering for special occasions is expected.

Residents in assisted living, memory care, and nursing receive three meals a day, and many of these meals may comply with a special diet as prescribed by the resident's physician.

Transportation

Typically, a community will provide bus and/or car service for scheduled trips to stores, medical facilites, church, social and entertainment events within a specified zone. Trips outside of the zone may be availalve for a fee.

Urban communities may have convenient public transportation and be within walking distance to stores and services.

Facilities

Facilities is one of the largest organization in a community. It provides housekeeping service at scheduled intervals to pamper the residents. Additional services such as moving furniture, upholstery cleaning, and picture hanging are available at extra cost, usually on a time and material basis.

Maintenance and repair of appliances, plumbing, and other core components in the living unit are included in the monthly fee. However, residents are responsible for maintaining substitutions and additions that they make. The care of the facility's infrastructure, common areas, and landscaping is significant. There is often an unseen custodian crew keeping the building interiors spotless.

Wellness and Preventive Care

Keeping healthy requires being active and exercising one's mind and body. Life plan communities fully understand this and place an emphasis on their wellness programs to keep residents active.

A community's wellness programs assist residents with their physical, intellectual, nutritional, and healthcare needs. There is also an abundance of social and entertainment programs, with many arranged by the residents' committees and groups.

Wellness and Fitness Programs Benefits

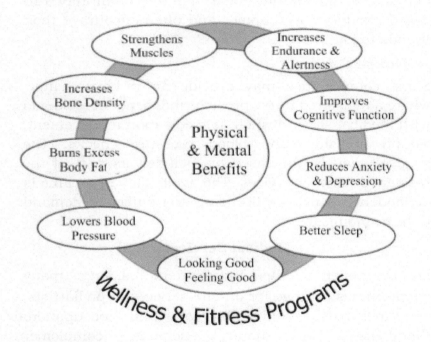

Figure 4.2 Benefits from Wellness and Fitness Programs

Wellness programs typically include a fitness center with treadmills, elliptical machines, cycles, rowing machines, and weights or resistance machines. Most residents have a pool for aquatic exercises and a bench for stretching. Instructor-led exercise for strength and balance may include tai chi, Pilates, yoga, line dancing, and chair exercises. Fair-weather activities may include periodic walks outside or in parks. There will be a wellness coordinator to assist residents. Upon request, the coordinator will tailor a health-maintenance program to an individual's ability and need.

Some communities may have shuffleboards and tennis courts, and a rare few have golf courses. The fitness facilities are key to the quality of life for residents and to keep older adults engaged in the community. Engaged residents are happier and often encourage their friends to join them.

In-House Clinic

Some communities may provide an in-house clinic, where a registered nurse provides independent residents with medical services such as medication management, wound dressing, and blood pressure checks. The services may be fee-based or included as part of the resident's normal services. The availability of a clinic is dependent upon state licensing and sufficient demand to be economical.

Medical Services

For the benefit of their independent residents, many communities arrange for on-site services of podiatrists, acupuncturists, and physical and occupational therapists. The therapy services complement independent living, as well as their assisted living and nursing services; however, a doctor's order may be needed to use some of these services.

In-Home Care

Some communities on their own or through arrangement with an agency provide trained and certified personal-care aides/assistants (PCAs) to assist residents living in independent accommodations with their daily living activities, such as bathing, dressing, grooming, and transferring in and out of bed. While PCAs are not licensed to administer medication, they may provide reminders and hand medication to their clients. A PCA's responsibility may also include housekeeping (making beds, doing laundry, washing dishes), preparing meals, and running errands for his or her client.

Occasionally there is sufficient demand among residents in a community to provide part-time care on a scheduled basis between two residents or more at a lower cost per person.

The resident will bear the full cost as it is not part of the standard service for independent residents. However, some residents prefer in-home help, either temporarily or permanently, rather than moving into assisted living. Residents may make their own in-home care arrangements if the service is not available through their community.

In summary, independent resident have alternatives in meeting their health-care needs.

Continuum of Care

A community's health center provides assisted living and skilled nursing services on a temporary as well as long-term basis. Most communities proivde memory care as well. The description of the health center's services and processes is extensive and is contained in Chapter 8, "The Health Center."

"I Can't Continue to Be Mary's Care Provider"

"Ray, you are no longer able to act as Mary's full -time caregiver," said his doctor. " You must get help or admit Mary to a suitable facility for her dementia. You are suffering from fatigue and extreme stress. Your high blood pressure and your fall from fainting should be adequate warning that your health is at risk... you're burned out! You cannot help Mary if you are ill or dead."

"Can't you prescribe some medication to get me over this?" exclaimed Ray Taylor.

"We are not dealing with a temporary situation. As you well know, Mary has Alzheimer's disease , and it gets progressively worse. Helping her cope with the disease is best handled by trained nursing aides."

"I cannot bear to be away from her and dump her in a nursing home."

"Traditional nursing homes were yesterday's solution. Today there are facilities, referred to as 'memory care ,' that are like assisted living, but specialize in treating patients with Alzheimer's and other forms of severe dementia. They provide a pleasant, safe, and nonthreatening environment for their patients."

"But then I would not be near her."

"Consider finding a memory facility with suitable housing for yourself within walking distance. Perhaps a better alternative is for the two of you to move into a life plan community, with you in independent living and Mary in the memory-care unit. Then you would be near her and be able to have a life of your own by joining the other independent residents in the various activities that are available to the community."

"Thanks for the advice. I'll check out the life plan community options," said Ray.

One Month Later

" Your blood pressure is near normal, and I'm glad to hear that you have not had a fainting spell since I saw you last," said Ray's doctor.

"I took your advice and now have a home aide coming in to look after Mary for three hours every day, " said Ray. " We are on a wait list at a community having a nice memory-care facility. They expect that there will be a vacancy for Mary within six months. They will hold a single apartment for me so we can move in together. Also, we have an offer from a neighbor to buy our house when we move out."

"That is great news," said Ray's doctor.

Four Months Later

When the day arrived, Ray Taylor picked up the keys of their apartment at Ocean View Manor. After checking out the apartment and assuring himself that the furniture that they intended to bring would fit, he went to the health center for advice on how to ease Mary into her studio apartment in the memory-care unit.

"Ray, it is important to stage the apartment with furnishings that Mary is familiar with, " said Dorothy Wells, the head nurse. " Bring her over alone on one of her good days and with one or two possessions that give her comfort. Plan on staying with her the remainder of the day. Have someone else bring over her clothing and other furnishings that she will soon need. Let us know a couple of hours in advance so we are prepared to greet Mary and attend to her immediate needs."

"Thanks for your guidance...I expect that Mary will be moving in in a few days," said Ray.

Commentary.

The Taylors' experience exemplifies the ordeal that a couple can go through to arrange suitable and convenient long-term care for a loved one. If they had already been residents in a life plan community, Mary could have been in memory care much earlier, and Ray would not have risked a physical and mental breakdown.

Breadth of Activities and Programs

There are many committees and groups from which to choose, such as those shown in Figure 4.3 for a typical community. The figure identifies the activities that are formally organized. Clicking on an image on the communiy's intranet (an internal website) brings up information on the associated group or club. In addition, there are ad hoc and informal groups associated with specific events or facilities, such as the crafts room, game room, and woodshop.

Most communities publish a newsletter or periodical on happenings within the community, scheduled events, administration announcements, and resident stories. The publication may be created by either the administration or residents. The style, length, and format will vary among communities. For example, a group of residents in my community, Mirabella-Seattle, publish a twenty-four-page monthly bulletin. It provides a good view of life within the community. A current copy is available from my website at http://agingsmartly.org.

Opportunities to be engaged

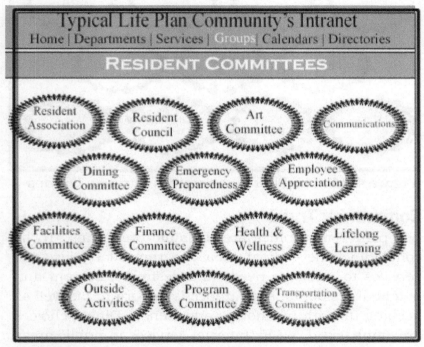

Figure 4.3.a. Life Plan Community's Intranet: Committees

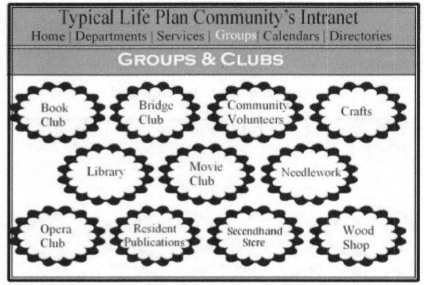

Figure 4.4.b. Life Plan Community's Intranet: Groups

Community Traits

Life plan communities are dynamic organisms. To be competitive they adjust their programs, facilities, and services to meet the needs and desires of current and potential residents. Appearance is important, as well as keeping up with technology and trends. Dining choices are emphasized. Wi-Fi/Internet services in public areas are routine. Some may have low-vision readers in their library, as well as hearing loops in their auditoriums.

There are an abundance of social and entertainment programs, with many arranged by the resident's committees. Many residents within a life plan community are also active volunteers in their extended community. Specific opportunities are dependent on the location, need, and availability of transportation. Typical activities include tutoring at a school, helping at a food bank, being a docent at a museum, and providing knitted articles of clothing for the needy, infants, and military personnel. The breadth and diversity of volunteer activity are greater in urban areas than in rural settings.

Congeniality

Personal images and attitudes are much different among seniors than they may have been in their earlier years. There is no need or desire to make pretenses or show off their achievements or wealth. Competition is no longer part of the game. The days of "boys with their toys" is long past. Rather than boasting about their past, they will offer their skill and experience when asked.

Not to be overlooked as a benefit to life plan community living is the abundance of like-minded residents to care about one another. Certainly, in a typical residential neighborhood, there will be one or two neighbors to assist you when you need help. But most will be occupied with their own families and making a living. Even your closest friends may not be there for you all the time.

In a community environment, residents are retired, so they are not concerned about making a living. They are accessible, perhaps next door or down the hall. They look out for one another.

Patience and Compassion

"Henry, I'm alarmed at the number of residents here with mobility problems," exclaimed Elise. "Have you noticed the number of walkers, wheelchairs, and canes around here? When there is an event, everything moves slow mo. And it is difficult to gracefully pass through with mobility-challenged residents side by side or chatting in the aisle."

"Well, it's definitely not what we expected in independent living," said Henry. "Especially given the rigorous examination of our physical and mental health as a condition for admittance here."

"And then there is Betty, the touchy-feely gal that wants to give everybody a pat or a kiss. I certainly wasn't expecting that and the number of infirm in our midst," concluded Elise.

Commentary.

It is not unusual for new residents to be alarmed by the number of physically and mentally challenged residents in independent living. After all, management put them through the drill of being healthy upon entry. Shouldn't most of the residents sharing the independent living facilities be equally as healthy? Marketing may not have been forthright about the occurrence of disabled residents. A lot of the marketing information is on active retirement programs and services, such as fitness centers, crafts, games, excursions, and both entertaining and intellectual programs. Left unsaid is the occurrence of those who can no longer avail themselves of many of these services.

Independent living in a life plan community differs from living in a stand-alone active retirement facility without a continuum of care. There is no provision in a retirement community to gradually transition from independent living to assisted living or nursing care, so their residents needing health care quickly move, rather than linger

In a life plan community, the transition from independent living to assisted living or long-term nursing care is usually gradual. The transition may take months or longer. In the meantime, they are among the independently living. Further, those who are in assisted living and nursing centers can continue to participate in the independent living programs and use the facilities to the extent that they are able. Spouses and friends often accompany and help the residents in health care to get to an independent program or the dining room.

Gradually new independent residents adjust to the occurrence of the impaired residents in their midst. As they mingle with them at meals and events, they begin to overlook their handicaps and appreciate what they can offer. For example, a mobility-challenged resident may be a delightful conversationalist. Successful living in a community requires patience, particularly when navigating the hallways and byways. When there is congestion, traffic is at half speed, and it may be difficult to quickly pass through without being offensive or bumping into a frail person and putting him or her at risk of falling.

The mentally challenged also require patience and compassion. Many have been reduced to a fraction of the cognitive ability that they had in their prime. Some residents will be in early stages of dementia, and others will be suffering from strokes.

Most residents, particularly those who have known a declining resident, will take those who are declining under their wing by comforting and assisting them while they are still in independent living and visiting them when they move into the health center.

Volunteering in the Extended Community

" Hi. I'm Peter Friedman , and this is my wife, Michelle," said Peter as he sat down at the dinner table. " We moved in a couple of months ago and are still finding our way around Harbor Shores."

"Welcome, and this is my sweetheart, Darlene. Next to Darlene is Janet Powers, followed by John O'Rourke," said Ted Summers as he gestured.

"Well, what are your first impressions on living at Harbor Shores?" asked Ted.

"Well, it is pretty much as we expected with regard to accommodations, programs, wellness, and fitness. The two pools and the aquatic programs are great. However, there is a void. I'm not getting a se nse of accomplishment," said Peter.

"What do you mean?" said John.

"Let me explain ... Before moving here, I owned a machine shop. It's a three -generation family business, handed down from my father to me and then to my son, Paul. When Paul took over four years ago, I stayed on as the troubleshooter and the idea guy for complex jobs. But now that robots and 3-D printers for manufacturing are taking over, I'm out of my element. So, I was hoping that there was something here where I could contribute and have a sense of accomplishment."

"Gosh," said Ted, "we have a dozen or more resident committees that should scratch anyone's itch, such as Dining, Lifelong Learning, Transportation, Programs, and others."

"There are so many, but yet so few! Many require specialized knowledge or skills that I don't have, such as Art, Health and Wellness, Finance, Communications. Other committees, such as Dining and Transportation, primarily mediate differences among residents and speak to management for the whole community. I don't have the interpersonal skills or interest to do that. Don't get me wrong : all of these committees are important and enrich our lives here. But I'm looking for something where I can get my hands dirty."

"You should talk to Jan Swenson, who is the resident volunteer coordinator, " said Darlene. "She is a matchmaker between residents who wish to volunteer and the area charities and agencies that need help. I'm sure that she can introduce you to an organization that needs your skills."

"Thanks; I'll give Jan a call in the morning."

Four Months Later

"I see that we get to dine together again," said Peter.

"Yes, it has been a while," said Ted. "I recall at the time that you were looking for an opportunity to get 'your hands dirty.' Have you found it?"

"I sure have," said Peter. "Jan hooked me up with the Arbor Lake Sailing Club that is a couple of miles west of here."

"I'm somewhat familiar with it. They have boats that can be rented out."

"Yes, but their public service project is providing free training to youths on how to sail.

"Any youth between the age of thirteen and seventeen is eligible. The boats they use for training are ten feet long and have a pull-up keel that allows the boat to be set on the deck for repair or stored during foul weather. The club has a fleet of twenty-five of them, so they are frequently raising and lowering boats out of the water. It is a two-man job to do this by hand.

"The assignment they gave me was to design and build a contraption where one man can transfer the boats between the dock and the water. I was able to accomplish this with leftover material from my family's machine shop, so there was no cost to the club . I'm tinkering with other improvement projects for the club.

"In return, they gave me sailing lessons, and I will be a volunteer instructor this summer. If you would like, I will take you and Darlene out sailing one of these days."

"Wow, we'll take you up on it. It is good to know that you found a project you enjoy," concluded Ted.

Commentary.

Upon retiring, seniors find various outlets to consume their time that was previously taken up in earning a living. They may become more immersed in established interests or find new ones. Many will have a desire or sense of obligation to give back to their community and share their good fortune. Often there is a desire to spread their knowledge, skills, and wisdom to those who are younger.

When people initially retire, they are generally aware of volunteering opportunities in their communities. However, when they move into a life plan community in a different location, they may need help finding an appropriate volunteering outlet.

Most communities have a coordinator or committee to help new residents identify programs that may be suitable. Nonprofit communities are implicitly obligated to have a volunteer program to legitimize their nonprofit status.

There are also opportunities within the communities for helping fellow residents, particularly those in assisted living, memory care, or nursing care. Visiting is appreciated, as well as assisting the activities director with group events.

Providing a helping hand either within the community or in the surrounding community can be rewarding and provide a sense of accomplishment for the residents who choose to do so.

Community Secondhand Stores

Most life plan communities have secondhand stores that will accept items that residents no longer want but still have value. Many of the donated items come from new residents moving in with more than they can use and items left over upon departure. Typical items donated are clothing, household goods, jewelry, wall hangings, electronics, and furniture.

Store volunteers separate the goods into items the store will sell, usable items for Goodwill, the Salvation Army, or local charities, and recyclable items. The store customers are residents, guests, and employees. Some stores may also sell to the public. Sale frequency and hours are situational based on the individual community's size, store and storage space, volunteer availability, and public accessibility. The extremes are daily openings to a once-a-year sale. My community, Mirabella-Seattle, has a store that is open daily, but only to employees, residents, and their guests. The picture is the entry to the Mirabella store.

The proceeds from the store go to a nonprofit 501(c)(3) foundation that benefits employees and residents, as well as local charities.

Collaborative Living

This is the glue that binds the residents to one another and to the staff. This is an important feature, not to be taken lightly. It has benefits and obligations. Like a commune, it implies one for all and all for one. Life in a community creates an esprit de corps like what is found in college fraternities, sororities, and military units. The residents, while having varied skills and experiences, share interests and concerns in their retirement and twilight years. A good community will provide an abundance of activities and programs to keep the residents engaged with one another.

By necessity, a community consists of two layers of government. There is the management level, which may be a nonprofit or a for-profit corporation. Typically, this is the organization that planned, arranged financing, developed, marketed, and is now managing the facility. It is a complex business, requiring a breadth of skills and experiences.

Augmenting the management layer is the resident association, which typically consists of several resident committees that report to a resident council. The council aggregates resident concerns and needs for presentation to the life plan community's management. In a well-functioning community, there is a symbiotic relationship. The committees and council digest the concerns and suggestions of residents, filter the substance from the noise, and present the results to management. Management is relieved from dealing with the minutiae, and the committees and council have the satisfaction of participating in decisions.

Conveniences

It is often said that the whole is greater than the sum of the parts, and that is true regarding life plan communities. The parts include independent living accommodations; social, hobbies, and wellness programs; local transportation; and assisted living, memory, and nursing care.

The added value is the convenience of having all the services on the premises and providing a single management team. Handoffs among different levels of care are coordinated in-house.

Charitable Foundation

Many life plan communities sponsor a charitable foundation for the benefit of those within their community and the surrounding neighborhood. The foundation may be a separate nonprofit 501(c)(3) or be sponsored by its own nonprofit community. The nonprofit status exempts contributors from income tax on their contributions. Many foundations allow residents to identify specific program(s) to receive their donations. Unspecified donations go to the general fund. Grants may include the following:

+ Aid to residents outliving their financial resources without fault of their own. While those with a life-care contract will continue to receive the services of the community, they may need monetary help for clothing, dental/medical care, and incidentals. The community's charitable foundation will fill the gap

+ Scholarships for worthy employees

+ Emergency aid for employees in time of need

+ Equipment, programs, and services to enhance the lives of residents in the health center

+ Art and other decorative or landscaping objects to enhance the facilities and grounds

+ Financial support for outside community programs and local charities supporting the homeless, youth programs, and individuals on hard times, as well as training for volunteers supporting the community

+ General fund where allocations are determined by the foundation's board

Fund-Raising

Typically, a foundation makes an annual fund appeal following publication of the previous year's annual report. In addition to a financial statement, the report usually identifies the year's grants and perhaps contains stories or pictures of recipients. There may be a kickoff event with drinks and hors d'oeuvres and possible entertainment. The fund-raising drive may last a month or so, followed by a concluding event.

Some communities have legacy programs that accept end-of-life bequests to the foundation. Bequests may be in the form of a charitable remainder trust, life insurance, or an IRA benefit.

Summary

In this chapter, you have learned about a community's living accommodations and its residents' benefits and services. Social and wellness programs were covered, as well as facility services, transportation accommodations, and health services. Resident participation and group activities were described with an awareness that some of the communities need space and patience in handling their walkers and wheelchairs.

Chapter 5

Life Plan Community Landscape

Life plan communities may be on a multiacre campus in a rural or low-density suburban setting or in a multistory building or buildings in an urban or high-density suburban setting. A typical community has separate areas for independent living, assisted living, memory care, and a health center with skilled nursing care and therapy. Common areas include a lobby, dining areas, library, exercise rooms, pool, auditorium, conference rooms, crafts area, and perhaps a woodshop.

Life Plan Community Characteristics

Life plan communities come in all sizes, origins, and management structure. Today there are nonprofit, for-profit, cooperative, and faux life-plan communities. Valid life plan communities must provide assisted living, and skilled nursing services within or near their campus/building. Approximately three-fourths of life plan communities offer memory care as well.

Health services outside the campus need to be under contract and ideally within walking distance. Memory-care residents, having special needs, should reside in living units separate from the others.

Faux life plan communities fall short in providing all the health services. Prospective residents should confirm that all expected health services are in place before moving in. A community's ambiance, tempo, and breadth of service offerings will be influenced by its size.

Today there are nonprofit, for-profit, and a very few communities under cooperative ownership in states where it is recognized, such as New York. While most life plan communities are nonprofit organizations, for-profits are strong contenders and growing faster than nonprofits.

Nonprofit Life Plan Communities

Nonprofit life plan communities qualify for charitable status under IRS code 501(c)(3). This qualification is based on their mission to provide housing, health care, and financial security for the aged, allowing them to allocate all their operational income without taxation to the care of their residents. Another advantage that nonprofit life plan communities have is access to cheap, tax-exempt municipal bond financing that can be arranged through a state's housing authority.

Evolution of Nonprofit Life Plan Communities

Nonprofit life plan communities began more than a century ago under religious and affinity sponsorship. Often these were a spin-off from a nursing-home operation. Most are still under faith-based sponsorship. Faith-based affiliations account for about 85 percent of all nonprofit communities. Among this group about 83 percent are Protestant, 11 percent are Catholic, and the remaining are Jewish and other denominations. Lutheran, Methodist, and Presbyterian affiliations account for most of the Protestant communities.[23]

---

[23] Charts 4-14a, 4-14b, 4-14c and 4-14d, Affiliation by Systems and Units", 2016 LeadingAge Ziegler 150, https://www.ziegler.com/z-media/3215/2016-leadingage-ziegler-150-publication_final.pdf

Secular communities include those sponsored by universities, hospitals, government, military, and others.

The sponsors, mostly nonprofit organizations as well, start the process by seeing a need for a community, conducting a feasibility study, and arranging for financing, development, construction, marketing, and fill-up. Most engage professionals and specialists in the group housing industry to do the development and start-up. Upon completion, the sponsor may manage the facility or assign the management to an experienced for-profit or nonprofit organization. In either event, the sponsor will have a position on the community's board of directors. The life plan community will be established as a separate nonprofit 501(c)(3) organization, isolating the sponsor and management firm from financial liability. Most new nonprofits still use this approach today.

Economic Influences

The 1970s began a boom in nonprofit community development by using resident entrance fees for a significant portion of capitalization of the facilities' assets. This new business model allowed the sponsor/developer to use their own money only for planning the project and obtaining construction loans from the banks. Much of the financing came from the initial residents' returnable entrance fees, which paid off the construction loans and often reimbursed the developer for start-up costs.

The 2010 recession put the Life Plan Community's business model to a test with some communities teetering on bankruptcy. While there were few failures and displacement of residents, most of the communities under stress could refinance or were acquired by stronger firms. While there were very few residents displaced or lost part or all of their refundable entrance fee, the possibility was emotionally draining. The last thing that a resident wants to consider is moving again and possibly losing part or all of their refundable entry fee. I cover this in detail under "Weighing the Financial Risk" in chapter 12.

Information Sources

There is a wealth of readily available information on nonprofit communities from sources including:

+ **LeadingAge**, the dominant association for six thousand nonprofit providers in the field of housing and health services for older Americans.

+ **GuideStar**, which provides financial data derived from IRS Form 990 filings by all nonprofit organizations. Its database can be searched by name, location, or type of organization.

+ **CARF-CCAC**, the Commission on Accreditation of Rehabilitation Facilities and the Continuing Care Accreditation Commission are the accrediting commissions that identify the life plan communities meeting their financial and service standards. Both for-profit as well as nonprofit communities can apply for accreditation.

+ **Ziegler**, an investment bank specializing in arranging financing for health-care facilities and senior housing.

+ **State organizations** that regulate life plan communities. They are likely to be the organization regulating assisted living, boardinghouses, nursing facilities, and senior housing. The specific governing agency regulating these communities varies greatly among the states. It may be the departments of health, social/senior service, insurance, or others.

+ **CMS**, the Centers for Medicare & Medicaid Services monitors and rates all skilled nursing facilities, including those in life plan communities.

For-Profit Life Plan Communities

Prior to 1984 there were few for-profit life plan communities, even though there was an abundance of for-profit senior retirement, assisted-living, and nursing-home communities. The owners of these other business types gradually moved into the life plan community market as well. Hotel operators like Hyatt joined in with luxury communities that began in California and Florida. Today for-profits account for 22% of the Life Plan Communities; up from 18% in 2009[24]. Further, most of the newly constructed communities continue to be for-profit. The American Seniors Housing Association (ASHA) annually publishes a member list of its fifty largest owners and operators, but without any breakdown as to the type of housing being provided. For-profit communities offer contract plans similar to nonprofit communities, but with a greater emphasis on rental plans.

Organizational Structure

For-profit communities may be under private or public ownership. If privately held, communities may be

---

[24] 2009 & current Ziegler National CCRC Listing & Profile,

individually held or owned by a partnership, with some being limited liability companies (LLC). The publicly held for-profit organizations may be a corporation or real-estate investment trust (REIT). As with nonprofits, for-profits may be self-managed or managed by a company that may be either nonprofit or for-profit.

Many for-profits are multi-site managed, where a parent or management firm operates the community, but ownership of the property may be as a subsidiary, separately owned or leased to the operator. While you will be able to obtain operational financial information for the community, it may not reflect the financial state of the parent or management firm. Single-site managed communities are more likely to fully disclose financial information.

Publicly held communities are subject to Security and Exchange Commission (SEC) regulations. They are required to release quarterly and annual financial statements, known as 10-Q and 11-K reports, respectively. Further, they may periodically issue other releases. The earnings releases and summaries are routinely available from investment websites, such as MarketWatch, Morningstar, Zacks, and so on. The 10-Q and 11-K reports can be obtained from the EDGAR website.[25]

Comparing For-Profits with Nonprofits

One would expect nonprofit organizations, being mission driven for the betterment of society and having a tax advantage, would charge less than for-profit communities for their services. The argument is that

---

[25] EDGAR: SEC's Electronic Data Gathering, Analysis, and Retrieval System, https://www.sec.gov/edgar/searchedgar/companysearch.html

nonprofits are altruistic and focused on serving their clients, rather than being profit driven. Often this is the case, and many nonprofit community operators also provide affordable housing and community health care, albeit often with government subsidies. But the expectation is not always met. Poor management skills or excessive pay to directors and managers can dilute their effectiveness. Life plan communities are in a market-competitive world.

Most seniors intending to enter a life plan community will consider only one or two locations. I'd advise them to consider both for-profit and nonprofits within their preferred locations. Even if a for-profit community is more expensive, other considerations may offset the difference.

Life Plan Communities' Place in Senior Living

Even though there are approximately four hundred thousand residents in two thousand life plan communities, such communities only accommodate 3 percent of seniors seventy-five-years old and older. If these communities are so great, as I have portrayed earlier, why do they only have 3 percent of the seniors in their targeted age group? I believe there are four reasons. Many seniors do not want to confront their mortality and are unlikely to plan ahead. A move-in is initially disruptive and costly. Most communities are priced at market rate and, as such, not affordable for many. And finally, many seniors have an irrevocable intent to age at home. The industry is beginning to recognize that "continuing care" is frightening and a hard sell. They are now emphasizing the social, physical, and active elements of their communities.

Life Plan Communities Locations

Ziegler Capital Markets, a specialist in senior living finance, published in 2009 a comprehensive list and profile of 1861 CCRCs in the United States[26]. Their criteria is that continuing care retirement communities provide independent living and nursing services. Ziegler omitted the requirement of assisted living even though most of the communities may have also provided assisting living. As a life plan community resident, I considered this to be a glaring omission.

I began a search for a complete list of communities without success. There are partial lists of communities and providers from LeadingAge-Ziegler, American Senior Housing Association (ASHA), GuideStar, CCRC.com, CARF-CCAC, Medicare, and state regulators. From these sources, I've compiled a list of 2,250 candidates and have willowed it down to 1,650 communities having independent living, assisted living, skilled nursing service and an internet presence.

There were two considerations regarding the internet requirement. Communities with websites are easy to find if you have a name and location or a link from a listing. Once opened, you can determine the services being offered without a lengthy phone query. Secondly, an internet presence is relatively inexpensive and an essential tool for marketing a multifaceted service. The absence of a website may suggest the lack of overall skills and personnel to deliver quality services.

My list of life plan communities is accessible from my website at http://agingsmartly.org. Once on the site

---

[26] "Ziegler National CCRC Listing and Profile", Senior Living Research, Ziegler Capital Markets, 2009

select the "FIND COMMUNITIES" tab for the mapping tools that allows users to select regions, zoom in to specific communities of interest and activate a community's website to peruse the community's layout and services.

The Concentration of Life Plan Communities

In the United States, housing and traditional health-care providers, such as hospitals, assisted living, and nursing centers, are generally dispersed evenly with the local population. However, in the case of life plan communities, the ratio of communities to population varies greatly among the states.

From my website's list of life plan communities, Figure 5.1 shows the number of communities by region and state. Note that Alaska and Nevada have no communities, and at the other end of the spectrum, Kansas has 70 and Iowa 67 in comparison of an average of 35 for all states.

More relevant is the number of communities' base on senior population. Figure 5.2 shows the number of life plan communities per 100,000 seniors, age 70 and older. The average ratio per state is 6.4. In comparison, Kansas is 27, South Dakota 25, Iowa 24 and Delaware 19, respectively. Ohio, New Hampshire and Pennsylvania follow at 14, that is over twice that average for all states. States well below the average are Georgia, New York, Vermont, West Virginia, Alaska (0), Hawaii, Nevada, Utah, Wyoming, Louisianan and Mississippi.

Number of Communities per State[27]

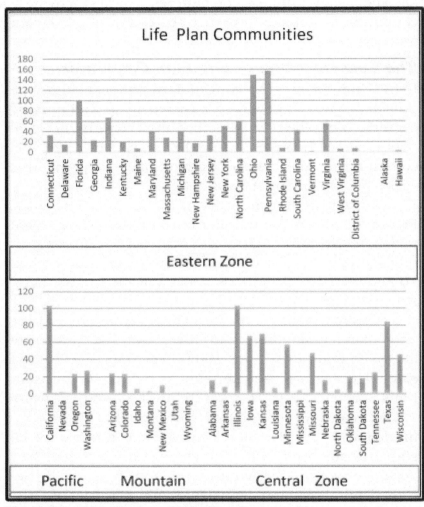

Figure 5.1. Distribution of Life Plan Communities

[27] "Compilation of listings from Ziegler, CCRC.com, GuideStar, CARF-CCAC, Medicare, and state regulators.

Disproportionate Distribution among States [28]

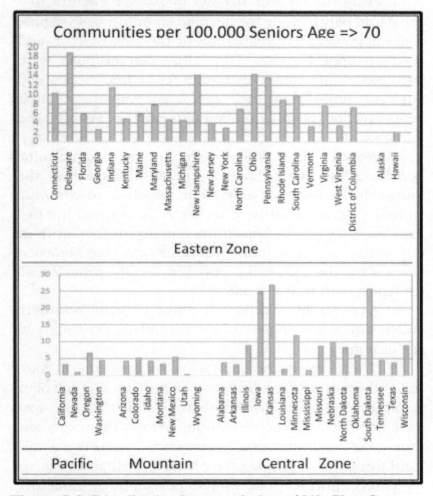

Figure 5.2. Distribution by population of Life Plan Communities within the United States

---

28 28 "Figure 5.1 data and "Table 2, Population by Age & Sex: 2000 and 2010," US Census /Age and Sex Composition 2010, https://www.census.gov/prod/cen2010/briefs/c2010br-03.pdf

What accounts for this density disparity? Factors that come into play include the life plan communities' origins, climate, government regulation or the lack thereof, and start-up opportunities. The initial communities were faith based, starting with homes for retired clerics and later accommodating their senior congregations. Their concentration began and remains in the eastern and middle states.

Notice that there are many communities bordering the Great Lakes, otherwise known as the Snowbelt. Seniors not able to or reluctant to continue shoveling snow and driving on ice in the winter have two choices. They can be snowbirds and live in the South in the winter, or move into a community where someone else clears the sidewalks and the facility provides all transportation that is needed.

Conversely, seniors in mild-climate southern states with a low density of communities may decide to age at home.

There are several anomalies. As pointed out, Kansas and South Dakota have the highest ratio of life plan communities yet their neighboring states to the west have none or a miniscule amount. Why is there very low number of communities in the western states? Is it a cultural thing where people prefer to fend for themselves, or regulatory hurdles that make development difficult? Most prospective community residents gravitate toward a community where they live, have lived, or have family. As seniors, few will venture to unaccustomed areas without a reason. In many states, the choices are few and far between.

Density of Independent Living Units among States

The availability of independent living units within a state is dependent on the state's senior population as well as the number of independent living units in the life plan communities. Two charts show the distribution of independent living units among Life Plan Communities identified in the 2014 LeadingAge Ziegler 150 report.

The sample includes 627 multisite and 100 single site communities, that is about half of all life plan communities.

Note that Figure 5.3 shows a normal distribution of independent living units (ILUs) among single-site communities as you might expect. However, Figure 5.4 for the multi-site communities show a preponderance of multi-site communities having fewer ILUs. The multi-site nonprofit providers have significantly smaller communities in comparison with single-site providers. The average community size for multi-site providers is 167 in comparison with 337 for single-site providers. In comparison my community, Mirabella Seattle, has 289 independent living units.

A possible explanation for low ILUs is that many multi-site providers may have two or more close-by communities where they share a common skilled nursing facility with sufficient beds to be economical. Or they may outsource their skilled nursing service to nearby facilities.

My personal view is communities with less than a hundred independent living units may struggle to provide a full range of services for their residents.

There is a Normal Distribution of ILUs among Single-site Communities[29]

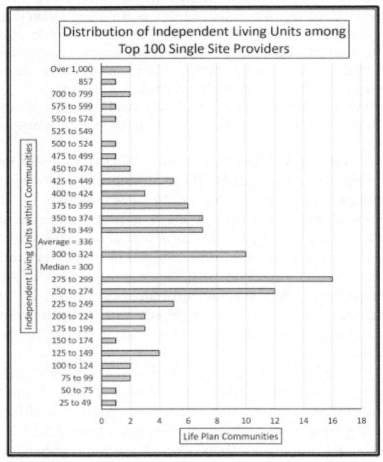

Figure 5.3 Distribution of ILUs among Single-site Providers

---

29 Based on "Table 6-1a, Single-Campus Senior Living Communities", 2014 LeadingAge Ziegler 150, https://www.leadingage.org/sites/default/files/LZ150-2014.pdf .

Multi-site Communities predominantly have less than 250 ILUs[30]

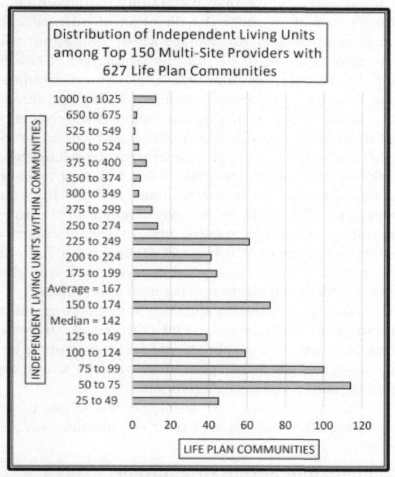

Figure 5. 4.. Distribution of ILUs among Multi-sites

---

[30] Based on "Table 3-1a, Multi-site Senior Living Communities", LeadingAge Ziegler 150. https://www.leadingage.org/sites/default/files/LZ150-2014.pdf . 2014

Scale and Complexity

Running a typical life plan community requires a large multifaceted staff under the direction of talented and experienced people. An average-sized community will have approximately 0.57 full-time employees (FTE) on staff if the site has its health center on campus. However, many employees, such as nursing and dining staff, are part-time, so the ratio of employees to residents will be quite a bit more. Many of the staff will be out of sight, such as laundry personnel and custodians who work mostly at night. Therefore, a five-hundred-resident community may have approximately three hundred employees. There will be a large variance in the ratio depending upon the relative size of the health-care center to independent living and other factors such as how much of the facility's maintenance and custodial work is contracted out to independent contractors.

The sponsoring organization may be for-profit or nonprofit, including secular and faith-based. Universities and hospitals may join as sponsors, an example being Evergreen Life Plan Community with the University of Wisconsin in Oshkosh, Wisconsin.

Many sponsors have several communities under their wing. The sponsor and their communities are referred to as an affiliation.

Ethnicity and Sexual Orientation

Expect most community residents to be Caucasian. However, all races are welcome, and some communities openly encourage diversity. I have never witnessed a problem where one's ethnicity, be it Irish, German, Portuguese, Jewish, Oriental, or African, is ridiculed. overall, residents in a community respect one another, even though they have different backgrounds.

Communities cannot discriminate based on sexual orientation. However, there are a few communities specifically for LGBT residents.

Summary

You have learned about the evolution of Life Plan Communities, their current organizational structure, and geographic differences in size. You've read about the distinction between nonprofit and for-profit communities and between multisite and single campus communities.

For names, locations, and Internet access to life plan communities meeting the continuum of care criteria, visit my website at http://agingsmartly.org.

Chapter 6

The Circle of Governance

Below are the participation entities having a role in the govenance and regulation of Life Plan Communities

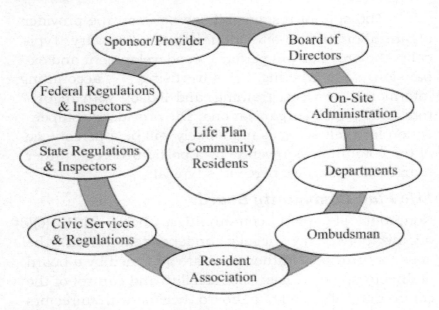

Figure 6.1. Circle of Governance

Life plan communities are complex entities with many moving parts and participants. Managing a community requires all the skills and processes associated with group housing, lodging, hospitality, and health services.

Sponsor/Provider

In the case of single-site organizations, the provider and on-site administration are usually the same. Single-site life plan communities account for approximately 40 percent of all the communities. The remaining 60 percent are managed as multi-site (system) communities.[31] Unlike nonprofit communities, for-profit communities will not have a community board of directors. Rather, a for-profit, being a corporation, will have a single board for all its operations.

The split of responsibilities between the provider organization and on-site administration can vary. Typically, the provider will perform site development and expansion, marketing, advertising, accounting, information services, training, and liaison with regulators and financial organizations. The providers' compensation for their services more likely will be a percentage of the community's revenue or a portion thereof, rather than a fixed fee. Five percent is typical.

Life Plan Community Board

Nonprofit life plan communities, being 501 (c)(3) organizations, are legally independent from their sponsor/provider. Rather, they are governed by a board of directors, which has responsibility and control of the community. Typically, a board begins with directors from or associated with the sponsor/provider. Once the community is established, there likely will be an effort to add some outside directors having ties with the local community. Over time it is possible that a resident or two will be appointed.

While the board has the power to change the community's direction and management, it is infrequently

---

[31] "Ownership/Sponsorship: Not-for-Profit & For-Profit," Ziegler National CCRC Listing and Profile, 2009

done and then usually limited to mismanagement or pending insolvency.

Reasons for a community board's reluctance to override management include the following:

+ Many of the board members are associated with the sponsor/provider.

+ The boards meet infrequently, and management controls the agenda and presentations.

+ Outside members , while well intentioned , may lack the skills and time to investigate and resolve problems.

On-Site Administration and Staff

Typically , the executive director , and perhaps other directors , are employees of the provider /sponsor . The remaining on-site personnel are employees of the community. On average there will be one-half full-time equivalent (FTE) employee for each independent living unit providing the services and functions identified earlier in chapter 4. The actual number of employees will be larger because many work part-time.

Many communities have quality control measures , such as periodic third-party resident and staff satisfaction surveys and peer level reviews among communities.

Table 6.1. Representative government regulations

Government regulations pertaining to Life Plan Communities	Independent Living	Assisted Living Memory Care	Skilled Nursing
LOCAL BUILDING CODES	√	√	√
FEDERAL BUILDING CODES			
• Americans with Disabilities (ADA) Accessibility Standards		√	√
• Standards of Health Care Facilities (NFPA 99)		√	√
• National Fire Protection Association's Life Safety Code			√
OPERATIONAL REGULATIONS AND CODES			
• Health Insurance Portability & Accountability Act (HIPA)	√	√	√
• Medicare's Skilled Nursing Facility Protective Payment System (PPS)			√
• SNF Resource Utilization Group - Version 4 (RIB-IV)			√
• Medicare Coverage Determination Manual			√
• Public Health Food Service Regulations & Inspections	√	√	√
• Yearly Inspections & Compliance Review, CMS Form HCFA_2567			√

Government Regulations

Local, state, and federal governments have roles in regulating a life plan community. In some cases, there is an overlap.

Local Regulations

Local governments have a hand in the design and operation of the physical facility. There are higher standards for buildings housing health centers than for multifamily residential buildings.

Most building codes are adaptations of the International Building Code (IBC). There are regional differences, such as the BOCA National Building Code in the northeastern states, the Southern Building Code in the southeast, and the Uniform Building Code west of the Mississippi. Likewise, each state or municipality may modify the code to their individual liking.

The municipal or county fire department will perform frequent inspections and be instrumental in establishing evacuation procedures. Many fire departments have well-staffed and trained emergency medical technicians to respond to calls for medical help.

State Regulations

Although many federal laws affect assisted living, the oversight of assisted living occurs primarily at the state level. All assisted-living and memory-care facilities, including those in life plan communities, are state regulated to a greater or lesser extent. There is no universal standard. The Department of Health is the regulatory agency in most states for assisted living. A few states assign the responsibility to their social and aging service departments. The specific regulations for each state can be found on the National Center for Assisted Living (NCAL) internet site.[32]

Also, among the states there is no uniform term for assisted living. Two-thirds of the states use the term "assisted living." Other terms used are assisted-care living facilities, residential care, boarding home, basic care facility, community residence, enriched housing program, home for the aged, personal-care home, and shared housing establishment.

Approximately forty states regulate independent living in life plan communities.[33] Regulations are through various agencies, with slightly less than half under the department of insurance. The remainder are assigned to departments of health, finance, aging, commerce/securities, and others. Typical, but not universal, regulations cover disclosure to state and residents, financial statements, escrow of entrance fees, monetary release from escrow associated with construction and sellout status, reserve requirements during operation, contract terms, residents' right to organize, liens, and so on.

---

[32] National Center for Assisted Living, "Assisted Living 2016 State Regulatory Review," June 2010, https://www.ahcancal.org/ncal/advocacy/regs/Documents/2016%20State%20AL%20Regulatory%20Review.pdf .

[33] Government Accounting Office, "Report to Special Committee on Aging, US Senate," June 2010, http://www.gao.gov/new.items/d10611.pdf .

Ombudsman

All states provide ombudsman programs that provide advocates for residents in nursing homes, assisted-living facilities, and other facilities providing long-term care for the infirm. The program's purpose is to protect residents' rights as defined in state and federal regulations. Upon receiving a request from a resident, family, friend, or other concerned person, the ombudsman investigates the situation and attempts to resolve any problems. Persuading the provider is the first step. Failing that, the ombudsman will report the incident to the regulators. Ombudsmen have open access to health-care facilities for investigating complaints.

The program began in 1972 under the federal Older Americans Act, but at the time was limited to nursing homes. In 1981, it was expanded to personal-care homes, including assisted living, memory care, and other facilities providing long-term care. The program's title is now "Long-Term Care Ombudsman Program (LTCOP)."

Ombudsman responsibilities as outlined in Title VII of the Older Americans Act are to

+ **Identify**, investigate, and resolve complaints made by or on behalf of residents;

+ **Provide information** to residents about long-term care services; and

+ **Represent** the interests of residents before governmental agencies and seek administrative, legal, and other remedies to protect residents.

+

Ombudsmen help residents and their families and friends understand and exercise rights that are guaranteed by law, both at the federal and state level. Typical problems may involve quality of care, use of restraints, transfer or discharge, abuse, and aspects of a resident's dignity and rights. Residents have the right to

+ be treated with respect and dignity;

+ be free from chemical and physical restraints;

+ manage their own finances;

+ voice grievances without fear of retaliation;

+ associate and communicate privately with any person of their choice;

+ send and receive personal mail;

+ have personal and medical records kept confidential;

+ apply for state and federal assistance without discrimination;

+ be fully informed prior to admission of their rights, services available, and all charges; and

+ be given advance notice of transfer or discharge.

Federal Regulations

Life plan communities need to be Medicare certified and proficient in the complex reimbursement process to recover their cost for their acute skilled nursing services. Very few communities offer nursing service without being Medicare certified.

Medicare exerts a lot of influence on how a nursing unit is run. For example, it prohibits a nurse from providing medical assistance to an outside person except in a dire emergency. Medicare annually inspects skilled nursing facilities that requires remedial correction, and reports their findings, which are made available to the public. Employee background checks and drug testing are mandatory for all employees who serve in facilities containing skilled nursing.

Fortunately, or unfortunately, depending on one's point of view, state and federal regulations often disallow the comingling of medical staff working between assisted living, skilled nursing, in-home care, and in-house clinic.

Resident Association

Most nonprofit life plan communities nurture and fund a residents' association that has the following purposes:

+ Provide a communications path for residents to convey their common needs and concerns to the staff, management firm, and board of directors.

+ Encourage residents to participate in programs and activities that benefit their fellow residents as well as the surrounding community.

+ Arrange cultural, social, educational, crafts programs and other pursuits.

+ Effectively enhance the quality of life for the residents and the greater community.

Resident Council

The association's council is its governing body. It typically consists of a president, vice president, secretary, treasurer, and a few at-large members who are elected by the membership. The council is the main conduit between residents and the administration on matters of common interest. It will speak for the residents on the budget and other important matters.

Resident Committees and Groups

Assisting the council are resident committees that deal with specific activities and services, such as health and wellness, transportation, facilities, communications, art, marketing, entertainment and lecture programs, welcoming, library, and continuing education. Committees that deal with community-specific services have the appropriate staff representative(s) attend their meetings.

Groups are informal organizations consisting of residents engaged in specific activities, such as sewing, card games, woodworking, dancing, and so on. Unlike committees, they are not governed by the Resident Council.

Bill of Rights Movement

Because of bankruptcies that occurred in the mid-1980s as well as during the recent great recession, many life plan community residents are concerned that their refundable entrance fees, being an unsecured debt, may be at risk should their community default on its financial obligations. While the actual number of residents who have been impacted over the years is very small, it is a valid concern.

In addition to financial stability and protection, residents would also like

+ the right to organize and advocate for themselves;

+ the right to be free from retaliation or intimidation when pursuing a resident's rights; and

✦ the means to enforce rights by a reasonable process.

A notable advocate for a bill of rights for community residents is Professor Katherine C. Pearson, who runs the Elder Protection Clinic at Penn State University at Dickinson School of Law. Also, the National Continuing Care Residents Association (NaCCRA) and some affiliated state organizations are actively pursuing bills of rights for their members. LeadingAge has cosponsored a bill of rights in Washington State and perhaps others. The states of New Jersey, California, Oregon, and Pennsylvania also have bills of rights to a greater or lesser degree.

Summary

From this chapter, you have learned about governing complexities of life plan communities. Their organizational structure is similar to a corporation with a board of directors, internal management, and often oversight and support from a sponsoring organization. Residents have their own ancillary organization governing their participation in the community. Government regulation includes local, state, and federal entities as well as Medicare and Medicaid.

Chapter 7

Life Plan Community Finance

Life plan communities face significant financial challenges in their beginning. The sponsors basically build full-service senior villages from the ground up. Facilities and services include housing, parking, transportation, dining, conference rooms, entertainment centers, pools, exercise equipment, and health-care facilities. Start-up costs include feasibility studies, planning and design, construction, marketing, and sales. Then they must hire a multifaceted staff before there is any revenue. Banks typically provide short-term loans for construction and perhaps more. But soon after the community is near or at full occupancy, refinancing takes place.

There are two approaches for a life plan community's long-term financing. The most common is to charge new residents a large refundable entrance fee to augment other sources of capitalization. This approach is used mostly by nonprofit communities and is the mainstay of the industry because most communities are nonprofit. The refundable entrance fees are unsecured, interest-free loans that are payable upon the resale of the occupant's apartment or cottage. Access to a large refundable entrance fee is possible because most community residents sell their home concurrent with moving in, and the sale proceeds are then used for entrance fees. While newer communities depend on resident fees for all their operating expenses and servicing of debt following construction and start-up, well-run older communities may reach the point in debt reduction where they can reduce resident fees or fund benevolent activities, such as providing some affordable living units.

In return for their entrance fees and a monthly service fee, residents receive the lifetime use of a designated independent-living apartment or cottage and accessibility to a continuum of care in the life plan community's assisted-living, memory-care, and skilled-nursing facilities. The incremental monthly cost for the health-care services is determined by the residence care agreement that is the operative contract between the resident and the community. Know exactly what is in the agreement before you commit to moving into any community.

Well-capitalized for-profit life plan communities, such as hotel chains or self-funded properties, do not generally use refundable entrance fees.

Payment Plans

The fee structure for most life plan communities consists of two components: a recurring monthly fee and an entrance fee. These fees will vary depending upon the type of contract chosen. Many communities offer two or more of the following payment plans. A few communities offer only one choice. The entrance fee can be nonrefundable, partially refundable, or fully refundable if a resident changes out shortly after moving in.

Type A, Life-Care Contract

This is also known as an all-inclusive plan. The entry and monthly fees cover all levels of care for life, whether the resident is living independently, in assisted living, memory care, or long-term care in skilled nursing. In addition to the cost associated with independent living, the fee includes the equivalent of an insurance premium for future health-care costs so there is no increase in cost when a higher level of care is needed. However, the standard monthly fee increases with inflation.

Because the community is committed to providing health service at the independent rate, they are very wary of accepting applicants who are not in good health when they enter independent living. Their screening process is like an insurance company providing long-term care policies.

Type B, Modified Contract

This is also known as a blended life plan. These contracts include some of the projected resident health-care costs in the independent living monthly fees. The remaining future health-care cost is covered by a higher fee than independent living only for the various levels of health care. For example, a community may charge a resident 50 percent of the market rate cost when residing in one of the special-needs facilities. Others may provide several free days in a health-care area before a surcharge applies. Or there may be other approaches. Doing a comparative cost/benefit analysis among blended communities is difficult because of the number of variables that may be involved. Prospective residents need to scrutinize these contracts thoroughly because reductions may only apply to some but not all health care or there may be a period before the subsidy begins.

Blended communities also screen prospective residents for apparent health issues, but will likely be less restrictive than the all-inclusive communities. They may also tailor a fee structure for prospective residents not meeting their normal criteria.

Note that the admissions criteria for both all-inclusive and blended communities are not static. They will likely fluctuate based on occupancy and the economy. In times of economic stress, such as the great recession (2008–2011), many communities reduced their entry requirements for the greater interest of reducing vacancies. Prior to that time, many had waiting lists even with tight entry requirements.

Type C, Fee-for-Service Contract

Type C à la carte contracts offer lower entrance and independent living monthly fees, but at the risk of larger long-term-care expenses. Health-care services are at the prevailing market rate at the time of need. Residents, however, do have guaranteed access to the community's health services.

Rental Contract

This is a month-to-month contract with a security deposit, such as the first and last month's fee. Health service will be at market rates without a discount. It is a pay-as-you-go plan, without the large entrance fee associated with the other plans. It is attractive to those without the means or desire to raise cash for a large entrance fee.

Most communities charging a rental contract are for-profit, whereas most of the communities mentioned above are nonprofit. Many rental communities fall short of providing a complete continuum of health care. Typically, in addition to independent living, they will offer assisted living or memory care. It is unlikely that a rental community will have a benevolent fund to assist a resident who cannot pay for their service. That said, their simplicity is appealing, and residents can easily move on without penalty or delay if they so choose.

As recently as October 2015, contracts were in the following proportions: Type A 33 percent, Type B 26 percent, Type C 28 percent, and Rental 13 percent.[34]

Communities providing Life Care Type A or Type B contracts use an actuarial process to determine their future health-care costs for pricing their contracts.

In conclusion, the health of prospective residents and to a lesser extent economic conditions will determine which communities are appealing.

Entrance Fees

A community may offer more than one entrance plan, with different ratios between the refundable and nonrefundable portions, such as a 90/10, 50/50, or a traditional plan, where all of the fee is nonrefundable. The entrance fee will diminish with the refundable component, but not proportionally. For example, if the entrance fee for a 95 percent refundable contract is $500,000, the fee for a traditional, nonrefundable contract may be 55 percent of the $500,000 or $275,000. The traditional contract may be advantageous to those who do not want to liquidate assets to raise the $500,000 or to younger people with long life expectancy. A traditional contract is not advisable for a couple moving into a life- plan community in their mid-eighties.

There is a slim possibility that a life plan community's refundable entrance fee may be considered a below market loan under Internal Revenue Code 7872. If so,

---

[34] Ziegler CFO Hotline.

the resident would receive a 1090 form for imputed interest.[35] There are lots of conditions and qualifiers that apply, such as the classification of the loan, does discounted present value apply, and periodic changes in the Internal Revenue Codes, that determine whether tax is due, its amount and whether it is covered by an exemption.

On the positive side, there is currently a medical expense tax deduction associated with a portion of the non-refundable entrance that is allocated for future medical services as explain following Monthly Fees

Monthly Fees

The recurring monthly fee covers the maintenance and upkeep of the resident's living area and his or her prorated share of the operational expense for all other independent-living services, such as food service, the wellness facilities, programs, resident services, upkeep of the common area, and administration.

---

[35] "Continuing Care Retirement Communities", Thomas D. Begley, Jr., Begley Law Group, http://www.begleylawyer.com/2010/05/continuing-care-retirement-communities-2/ .

Where your fees go.

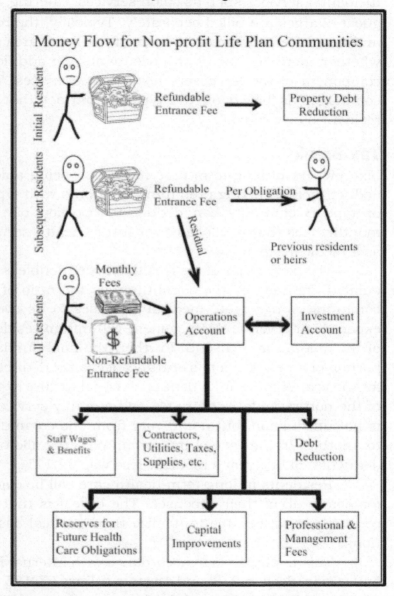

Figure 7.1. Money flow for nonprofit communities

Incidental services such as salon services, catering, and guest charges are billed separately. Typically, the room and board fee is based on the size of the living area and whether there are one or two occupants. An additional component of the fee covers health-care services. This component is based on the type of contract that the resident has entered.

Tax Break

Like owners of long-term care insurance being able to deduct their recurring premiums, residents with type A or type B contracts can deduct the portion of their monthly fees that is allocated for future health services as a medical expense.

The percentage of the fees that is deductible is calculated annually by the community as the ratio of the community's aggregate medical expenses to its overall expenses or revenue. Management will inform residents of the amount at year-end. Further, the nonrefundable portion of a new resident's entrance fee is tax deductible for the year of move-in. A deduction equal to 20% to 40% of the non-refundable entry fee and monthly service fee is not uncommon, but it can vary from one community to another. In the case of my community, the allowable deduction of last year's monthly fees was 32.12%.

Residents in long-term health care will be eligible for nearly all of their expenses. The caveat is that the residents must be able to itemize their medical deductions.

This tax break is in accordance with Internal Revenue Code, Section 213, and revenue rulings 67-185 and 76-481, PLR 8212102, and the federal tax case of Baker v. Commissioner.

Financial Considerations

The financial   state   of a life plan   community is important to both current and prospective residents . Selecting a community should be viewed as a lifelong decision. Residents expect consistent living conditions and continuation of all the services offered at move-in, including   health -care   services . Fees should be reasonable   and competitive   and the premises   well maintained.

How Resilient Is the Community?

Most communities are financially resilient , but during times of economic stress , weak operators will struggle , and some will go into bankruptcy . A 2009 Government Accounting   Office (GAO) study probed the financial risks facing the industry .[36] A life plan community 's financial
difficulties can lead to unexpected increases in fees and vacancies . In the case of a community   's failure , residents could lose part or all of their entrance fee and in rare circumstances   be forced to leave , the GAO report stated. It concluded that state regulators need to be vigilant in their efforts to help ensure   adequate consumer protections for residents of communities.

While the actual number of community bankrupt - cies or reorganizations   during   the 2008 great recession was very small , it nevertheless   was a very traumatic experience for those residents impacted

---

[36] "Government Accounting Office, Continuing Care Retirement Com-munities Can Provide Benefits, but Not Without Some Risk," 2010, http://www.gao.gov/products/GAO-10-611 .

by it. A few residents were displaced, and more suffered some financial loss.

Yet little has been done at the state level in this regard. The few bright spots where states have intervened on behalf of life plan community residents are identified in chapter 6 under the "Bill of Rights Movement." Until more is accomplished, current residents must be watchful and vocal if they observe a problem. With some digging and persistence, future residents, in conjunction with their financial advisers, can obtain sufficient information to make an adequate assessment of a community's financial condition.

If financial stress causes a community to deteriorate and become intolerable, there will be a large emotional cost whether residents stay or move out. Residents who decide to move will lose the support and friendship of the community to which they have become accustomed. Further, they may lose part or their entire refundable entrance fee or must wait an indeterminate time for payment. Should they decide to move into another life plan community, they will incur the cost of new refundable and nonrefundable entrance fees. There will be the added cost of the move and possible temporary lodging. Further, there may be a difference in health-care coverage between the sites.

The residents who wait out the turmoil until the community is stabilized by either refinancing or takeover by another operator may experience higher recurring costs, a difference in continuing health-care services, and perhaps a loss of some of their original entrance fee. If a stronger and more experienced operator takes over, the change may be beneficial in the long run.

In the case of bankruptcy of for-profit communities, there will usually be the loss of the smaller entrance fee and the cost of temporary lodging and moving to a new facility.

Determining the financial condition of a community is covered in Chapter 12, Confirming Financial viability.

Summary

You have learned in this chapter the nuance of Life Plan Community finance with the variety of payment plans having different entrance fees and rebates. We've covered how a community is initially financed and often refinanced by using the residents' refundable entrance fees as collateral. You've seen a pictorial of how money flows through a community as it provides service to their residents. A tax break associated with life-care contracts is also covered.

Chapter 8

The Health Center

A life plan community's mission includes providing a continuum of health care consisting of assisted living, memory care, and acute and long-term skilled-nursing care as needed.

Health-Center Services

These health-care elements are generally managed as a set and often referred to as the health center. The director of the health center, in addition to being a health-care specialist, will also be well versed in the administrative role of complying with state regulations associated with the assisted-living and memory-care units and federal Medicare regulations governing the skilled nursing unit. The skilled nursing facility does not provide walk-in service. The admission process is formal and requires a doctor's orders describing the care to be provided. And attention is paid to the process of billing and receiving prompt payment.

Separately for independent residents, a community may have an in-house clinic providing nursing services such as wound care and administration of intravenous (IV) medications.

The health-care center is staffed by licensed medical personnel consisting of registered nurses (RNs), licensed practical nurses (LPNs), and many certified nurse assistants (CNAs).

Most nursing care is temporary for recovery from falls, accidents, curable diseases, and surgery. Those in long-term nursing care require medical attention that is not available in assisted living or memory care.

Ideally a community would like to provide seamless health care to its residents for all their needs. But they are often hampered by state and federal regulations on how and when these services are available. Some services are available to all residents, and others are not without a formal transition between the levels of service. Thus, there are both hard and soft boundaries in the application of health care among residents. Further, there are variations among communities, depending on the government jurisdiction that they are in and the value-added features they offer. This section is intended to explain the services, regulatory constraints, and choices that communities have in fulfilling their commitment to a continuum of health care.

Assisted Living within the Community

Assisted living is available for residents who need assistance with activities of daily living (ADLs), but do not require constant care. The need for assisted living usually develops gradually, so there is time for planning the transition from independent living.

A life plan community's assisted-living facility is generally separate from independent living, such as on a separate floor or in another building, yet within walking distance to accommodate visiting by a spouse and friends. The living units are studios or one-bedroom units with the resident's own furnishings and belongings. There may be two-bedroom units for couples and possibly a kitchenette, even though all meals are furnished and either delivered to the resident's unit or available in a common dining room. There is likely an activity room as well.

In lieu of a separate facility for assisted living, a few communities provide assistance in the resident's independent units. The availability of remote monitoring makes this possible, but there are pros and cons. From the provider's point of view, they save the cost of a separate facility, but with a higher labor cost for aides traveling between apartments or cottages. They also must equip the living units with call buttons and supplies and may have to modify some living units to ADA standards to accommodate walkers and wheelchairs.

Residents requiring assistance may prefer staying in the living units to which they are accustomed. However, their spouses, while relieved of the physical aspects of providing care, will still be emotionally engaged and find it difficult to have a life of their own.

While I have included communities providing assisted living in their homes in my website, I'd advise prospective residents considering this arrangement to think it through before moving in. It is unclear whether a state's regulatory safeguards for assisted-living facilities, such as ombudsman visits, would apply to an aide at home.

Memory Care within the Communities

The 2017 LeadingAge-Ziegler report states that 77% of its nonprofit communities offer memory support, that may be in asssited living, skilled nusing or a specialized memory-care unit. Sixty percent of the communities have separate memory-care units. Life plan communities comprised 54% of the ccommunities in the survey. Otheres in the survey were independnet living,assisted living and nursing communities. The survey did not state the specific percentage having exclusive memory-care unis for each category, so it is not known whether life plan communities were above or below the 60% average. In compiling my list of life plan communities for my website, I observed more than half advertised memory support.

Prospective residents in a life plan community need to scrutinize the type of care being provided to a community's dementia residents. Also, inquire about a community's procedures for knowing where their patients are and what they do if someone is missing.

Some communities combine dementia patients with their assisted-living patients if there are not enough dementia patients to warrant a separate facility. This puts an additional burden on their staff, who must intervene when conflicts occur between the two types of patients.

Skilled Nursing Facility (SNF)

The skilled nursing facility provides twenty-four-hour nursing care and rehabilitation services to people with illnesses, injuries, or functional disabilities. Some residents may have a short-term need, perhaps caused by a fall or broken bones, that necessitates a brief hospitalization followed by rehabilitation in a nursing home. Other individuals may have more long-term needs or require care on an ongoing basis. Physical and occupational therapy will be available on-site or arranged locally with transportation provided.

However, not all communities have Medicare-certified nursing on-site. There are three alternatives for these communities to meet their obligation of providing nursing service as a part of continuum care. Many communities with nearby affiliates consolidate their nursing service at one location and provide resident transportation to and from the selected location. Others contract out nursing service to a nearby nursing facility. Finally, a few may provide nursing service without relying on Medicare payments.

Nursing Room Accommodations

Newer and recently renovated life plan communities will likely have private rooms for their residents in their skilled nursing facility. There is a trend toward single/private rooms that is influenced by factors such as infection control, error reduction, and patient safety and privacy. Countering this trend is the reluctance of Medicare and Medicaid to pay extra for single occupancy.

However, not all communities have Medicare-certified nursing on-site. There are three alternatives for these communities to meet their obligation of providing nursing service as a part of continuum care. Many communities with nearby affiliates consolidate their nursing service at one location and provide resident transportation to and from the selected location. Others contract out nursing service to a nearby nursing facility. Finally, a few may provide nursing service without relying on Medicare payments.

Conclusion: The Centers for Medicare & Medicaid Services' ratings speak well of life plan communities, with 66 percent of their communities scoring four or five, versus 45 percent of the other nursing facilities. However, only 1,537 out of over two thousand communities are Medicare-certified.

There are three alternatives for the remaining communities to meet their obligation of providing nursing service as a part of continuum care. Many communities with nearby affiliates consolidate their nursing service at one location and provide resident transportation to and from the selected location. Likewise, others contract out nursing service to a nearby nursing facility. Finally, a few may provide nursing service without relying on Medicare payments.

Medicare and Medicaid Service Ratings

Life plan communities have reason to be proud of their skilled nursing services, with 65 percent of their communities scoring four or five versus 47 percent of the other nursing facilities. (See "CMS Five-Star Rating System" in chapter 3 for a description of the rating system.) The distribution by the overall rating score for life plan communities and all other US nursing facilities is shown on the following page.

Table 8.1. Comparing Life Plan Community nursing facilities with others [37]

Nursing Facility Count and CMS Percentage Rating				
Overall Rating	Life Plan Communities		All Other Nursing Facilities	
	Count	Percent	Count	Percent
5	588	38.3%	3147	22.5%
4	421	27.4%	3180	22.7%
3	243	15.8%	2664	19.0%
2	219	14.2%	2820	20.2%
1	66	4.3%	2170	15.4%
Beds in Facilities	median	average	median	average
	75	87	100	108

Admittance into the Skilled Nursing Facility

Prior to a patient's admittance, his or her physician must provide written orders for the patient's treatment and medication. A physician will also supervise the patient's care for the duration of his or her stay.

Some communities will have a physician under contract to care for patients who do not have a personal physician.

Although a community's nursing staff is on-site twenty-four hours a day, drop-in services are not allowed for those residents without a physician's order. There are two reasons for this restriction. First, impromptu demand might disrupt scheduled care for patients. Secondly, it would create a cumbersome cost-accounting problem: nursing employees would have to clock out

---

[37] Data.Medicare.gov., nursing-home-compare.

from the SNF and then charge their time to a separate account to comply with federal Medicare cost-accounting rules.

Consequently, independent residents in the community need to obtain medical services at their physicians' office, a hospital, or an on-site clinic if available. The exception is in the event of a dire emergency, which usually should be handled by calling 911.

Medicare, Medicare Advantage, and HMO Coverage

Given that nearly all life plan community residents are initially covered by Medicare, the community's acute-care facilities must be Medicare authorized to provide economical services to their residents. Otherwise, patients without insurance would self-pay, or the community's fees would be exorbitant. However, Medicare coverage comes with strings attached. The most common conditions and exclusions of treatment in SNF are as follows:

+ Admittance requires a physician's written order.

+ Posthospital coverage applies only if the patient's hospital stay is three midnights or longer. (There have been a lot of vocal complaints among seniors about this three-night rule, and there is a possibility that Medicare will acquiesce and change it.)

+ Coverage will lapse after one hundred days.

+ Coverage will lapse if further improvement is unlikely. However, this rule will no longer apply if a federal judge approves a beneficiary/ government settlement.

+ Long-term custodial care is excluded.

Community residents who do not qualify for Medicare coverage can still be treated in the facility if they are formally admitted and meet any of the following conditions:

+ They belong to a Medicare Advantage program or HMO that has a contract with the community. Some advantage plans or HMOs may provide coverage on a case-by-case basis.

+ They have contractually signed up for long-term care in lieu of independent care and pay the agreed-upon rates in the community's residence care agreement.

+ They pay the daily rate for interim care. The rate will likely be less than the public rate. Be sure to inquire about the cost.

+ They qualify for free-stay days that are sometimes provided by the communities.

Hospice Care

Hospice care is available to residents under Medicare Part A. It is provided to seniors covered by Medicare Advantage programs, HMOs, and traditional Medicare. The program helps the terminally ill live comfortably at their location of choice by meeting their physical, emotional, social, and spiritual needs. Services include palliative care (relief of pain and symptoms), counseling, drugs, equipment, and supplies for the terminal illness and related conditions. Short-term respite care is also available for an at-home patient care provider.

Within a life plan community, hospice is available to residents in independent living, assisted living, memory care, or nursing care. Their location is not relevant. For a patient to be eligible, a doctor must certify that the recipient is terminally ill, with a life expectancy of six months or less. If the patient's health improves or the illness goes into remission, hospice care will cease. It can be restarted again if there is a reversal in the person's condition.

Community Clinic

Many communities have a health clinic for their independent residents who occasionally need the services of on-site or visiting medical professionals, such as:

✦ a nurse for a blood pressure check, injection, or dressing a wound;

✦ a podiatrist for foot care; and

✦ an acupuncturist.

Typically, this is a billable service rather than being covered by the standard monthly fee.

Transitioning into the Health Center

Entering assisted living or memory care is usually a planned event, as is access to skilled nursing for long-term care or scheduled surgery, such as a joint replacement.

Entering skilled nursing following a fall, accident, stroke, or other medical emergency is a traumatic event. Often the family or caregivers are unprepared for handling the situation. While these residents consciously selected the life plan community as their health-care provider in the event of need, their preparedness upon entry into the health-care facilities varies. Even though residents qualify for treatment in the community's health center, the actual process for admission can be cumbersome and confusing. Some residents prepare by

learning in advance the admissions process and the contacts that will help them in the transition. Other residents, to their detriment, decide to avoid the subject
until it is thrust upon them.

The following resident stories will explain common
practices for admission and the rationale behind them.
Many of the practices relate to how communities are reimbursed for their services. Since almost all the community health-care patients will have Medicare coverage
that covers most acute-care instances, the entry process
and follow-up wellness reviews will usually follow Medicare protocol or the protocol for Medicare Advantage or
Health Maintenance Organization (HMO) clients.

"Oh Lord, My Husband Was in a Car Accident."

Jane Nelson was distraught as she entered the
community's resident services office. "David was T-
boned in a car accident and is in the hospital with
multiple injuries, including a concussion, a broken
arm, ribs, and maybe a shoulder injury, " Jane
exclaimed to Barbara, the resident services manager.
" How do I get him admitted into our nursing center
when he is released from the hospital?"

"Jane, I'm so sorry to hear this and trust that David
will recover quickly, " said Barbara. " Arrangements for
his transfer here are made through Maurice, our
admissions director. It is a rather complicated
process, so get in touch with Maurice right away so
arrangements are complete by the time David is
scheduled to be released from the hospital. Maurice
will walk you through the process."

Soon After

" Jane, the hospital will assign either a social worker or discharge planner to coordinate David's transfer to us," said Maurice. " Have this person contact us by phone when David's release is scheduled. The coordinator will send us a clinical assessment of David's condition and the physician's orders. From your description of David's injuries, I expect that the hospital will want David transported here by cab ambulance, rather than by car. The coordinator should make the transportation arrangements for you. We are saving a bed for David. Here is a packet of information on what to expect when David is under our care."

"It says here that your treatment is based on the doctor's orders," said Jane. " Which doctor are we talking about...his personal physician or the hospital doctor?"

"It will be the doctor from the hospital that prepares the discharge papers. Most likely, he will be the doctor that has attended David throughout his stay in the hospit al. The hospital physician will inform David's personal physician of his condition and treatment if requested to do so. Our registered nurse will assess and report David's condition daily."

"Will physical therapy be required?" asked Jane.

"Most likely. If it is not in the initial orders, subsequent orders are likely and will be based on David's progress. As you may be aware, our health - care center can provide therapy, so there will be no need to transport David elsewhere. I assure you that we can take care of everything from here during David's convalescence."

"Will Medicare cover this cost?"

"Since this is a no-fault state, either the other driver's auto insurance or your own will be the primary payer. Medicare will be secondary payer. The social worker at the hospital can help you with the payment details. Is there anything else that I can help you with?"

"Not at this time. Thanks for filling me in," concluded Jane.

Commentary

As described in the above story, there is a set protocol for the admission of a patient from a hospital to an acute-care nursing facility. The process is the same whether the nursing facility is in a community or elsewhere. The doctor's orders govern the patient's treatment and rehabilitation plan. The nursing staff will provide feedback to the doctor. Often physical or occupational therapy will continue after the patient is released from nursing care. Communities with a therapy staff on-site can continue to provide treatment as needed under the direction of the patient's doctor.

"I'm Scheduled for Back Surgery Next Month."

Jake Hazer looked perplexed as he walked into Three Trees' skilled nursing office. "I'm having back surgery and have been told that I will take a couple of weeks or more to recover, and I'll need physica l therapy too, " said Jake. "My HMO Advantage coordinator is going to schedule this recovery at the Elliott Convalescing Center that is across town. I 'd like my recovery and therapy to be scheduled here, but he said the Three Trees is not a preferred provider for their plan. Why did I bother moving into this community if I cannot use the health services here?"

"To provide services to residents with HMO plans, we have to be preapproved by the plan administrators, " said Raymond, the health-center administrator. " Usually this approval is on a case-by-case basis. On occasion a p lan's administrator will provide us with blanket approval, particularly when we have several residents here under their plan and they become comfortable with our services. What is the name of your plan and your contact person? I will intervene on your behalf. Most of the time we are able to obtain approval to provide the convalescent and physical therapy services here. I'll keep you abreast of o ur progress."

"Boy, I sure hope this works out. I'm going to be really unhappy if not!" said Jake.

Commentary

Life plan community residents with traditional Medicare plans have the opportunity to select any Medicare-approved provider for their rehabilitation. Naturally, they will select their community's facility. However, HMO or Medicare Advantage plans will not cover the resident's cost unless the community has been preapproved. There are two types of approval. The most desirable is a blanket contract with the community where all of the HMO or Medical Advantage clients are automatically approved. If not, the community may obtain approval on a case-by-case basis. These approvals are not automatic and may not be timely. Prospective community residents who belong to an HMO or Medicare Advantage plan should inquire whether the community has a standing contract with their provider or has been able to routinely obtain approval. If you are scheduled for planned surgery, ask the health center to begin a preapproval request prior to your surgery date.

An additional complication with HMO contracts is that the HMO's treatment protocol and reporting requirement will likely be different than that for Medicare. This may be an additional burden on the community's staff.

Ed Wandered & Was Not Found until Morning.

Elizabeth Burnett was both relieved and dreading this meeting with the resident services manager. Surely her husband Edward's persistent wandering and getting lost had come to a head. She quickly noticed that the managers from security and health services were also in attendance.

" Beth, you could have lost your husband last night, " exclaimed Margaret Walsh, the resident services manager. " Edward was not found until early this morning, when a commuter noticed him shivering and in distress. The commuter called the police and kept Ed warm in his car until the police arrived. They, as well as some of our staff, were on the lookout for him all night. This isn't an isolated case of Ed's wandering. On the prior occurrences, we were able to locate him quickly. But winter is arriving, and another incident like last night could be disastrous."

"Thank God he was found soon," said Beth. "I won't let him out of my sight in the future. Aside from wandering, Ed functions pretty well."

"Your patience and love for him are laudable, but you cannot be there twenty-four-seven for him," said Jo Norton, the health services director. " Besides, you need a life of your own. Our assessment is that Ed is in early-stage dementia, which is manifested in his wandering and inability to find his way back home. Other symptoms of his dementia will soon follow. You need to consider promptly admitting him into our memory-care unit so we can provide appropriate care and the environment to treat his symptoms and keep him safe. I will set up a conference with you and Edward at your convenience to identify your concerns and our proposed care plan. I understand that you have a son and two daughters who live nearby. I encourage you to ask them to attend the conference as well. I expect that Edward is in denial of his condition, but he will likely be relieved to know that we can provide a suitable setting for him."

"Beth, during the interim period when Ed is still living in your apartment, let the security desk know when you are not within eyesight of him so we can be on the lookout for him, " said Robert Jacobs, the security manager. "His safety is our paramount concern."

Beth reluctantly agreed to have a family meeting with Jo Norton.

Commentary.

Committing a loved one to memory care is a wrenching experience. Patients with Alzheimer's and other forms of dementia progressively lose cognitive function. In addition to memory loss, patients are often moody and irritable. Their condition varies from time to time from poor to nearly normal. The question for the spouse or caregiver is when, rather than if, the patient will be admitted into custodial care and, more appropriately, into a memory-care facility. Most life plan communities have these facilities, but when should a resident make the transition? Often it will occur following a defining moment, such as being dangerously lost as in Ed's case.

More appropriately, when the spouse's dementia is in its early stage, the couple should arrange for entry into the community's memory-care facility when the disease reaches a predetermined criterion. Ideally, both the resident and spouse should jointly agree on the criteria. It could consist of several parameters, such as the inability to perform one or more activities of daily living (ADL), a failing score on a cognitive test, persistently getting lost, evidence of irrational behavior, and so on. Of course, the community's administration should be aware of the future need for admission and be kept abreast of developments, so they can accommodate the resident when the time of need occurs.

"They Say Judith's Condition Is Not Improving."

" Bob, we are sad to report that Judith has shown no measurable improvement over the past two weeks, " said Gloria Travis, the health center director. " Medicare requires us to continually report progress of all Medicare patients in rehabilitation. Their benefit period ends when progress stops or on the hundredth day, whichever comes first. As such, we are no longer able to bill Medicare for rehabilitation."

"What? I was never told this when Judith was admitted here. This is a real shock!"

"We apologize for not mentioning it. It is unusual for measurable progress to cease before the hundredth day. Judith was making good progress initially, so we were not concerned. Then it abruptly stopped."

"Where do we go from here?"

"Normally we would propose custodial care for Judith."

Bob Hiller frowned. "Do you mean long-term care?" sighed Bob.

"Yes. Miracles happen, but it is unlikely that Judith will ever be able to return to independent living. Our staff is currently assessing whether Judith has made enough progress for assisted living or whether she needs to stay in the skilled nursing unit. You could consider continuing physical or occupational therapy here for Judith whether she is in assisted living or in skilled nursing. However, you will have to cover the full cost of the therapy. There has been some anecdotal evidence showing some benefit, but as far as I know, it has not been statistically validated. Before you pursue this path, you should consult with one or more specialists."

"I'll have to think about that."

"I'd like to schedule a care conference with you and Judith within a couple of days. You may invite family members or an advocate of your choice. At the conference, we will propose a plan to address Judith's continuing needs."

"How much is all of this going to cost?"

"What is your contract type?"

"We are under the modified, Type B."

"Whether Judith is in assisted living or skilled nursing, the member rate of the Type B contract is approximately 50 percent of the market rate. The specific amount for this year is shown in the resident handbook. There may be additional charges for incidentals."

"I'm glad that we had the foresight to enter a community when Judith and I were in good health. I know that Judith is in good hands and the costs are manageable. We have long-term care insurance that should cover the half that we are responsible for. I can't imagine the trauma in dealing with this situation without being here."

On the Cusp of Needing Care, But in Denial

Ring...ring. "Hello, this is Patricia Meyers."

"Ms. Meyers, this is Frances Taylor, the resident services coordinator at Greenhaven, Orlando. I'm calling about your mother, Betty."

"Is she OK?...Has something happened to her?"

"No, no...she is OK for now. However, I'm calling to schedule a care conference to discuss some behavioral and health problems that have been observed and to get an agreement on how they should be addressed. Our staff at Greenhaven questions whether Betty is still independently capable of making good decisions and carrying through with them."

"Gosh, I haven't seen her in over a year; but when I talk to her, she says that she is fine, has friends, and is having fun."

"Well, she is good at confabulation, but we are more concerned about hygiene and clutter issues that put her at risk of a fall or illness. Also, Betty often misses meals or does not eat balanced meals. While friends and neighbors are looking after her, it is not their place to do so.

"We have suggested that she consider moving into assisted living and possibly memory care, but she is adamant that she can continue to live independently.

"We are scheduling a care conference to decide on how to proceed. As her daughter with durable power of attorney, it is important for you to participate. I know that you live a good distance from here. We would like you to be present at the care conference, but I can arrange a telephone conference if you cannot be here. Are there other family members who can attend or be conferenced into the call?"

"Can you force her to move?"

"No, but I expect that you and possibly other family members can convince her to move into assisted living once you hear all of the observations from housekeeping and other staff members. You may also appoint an advocate to represent her at the conference."

"What if the family decides she can remain in independent living?"

"For her safety and the welfare of the rest of the community , we will likely require that she have at her expense a care provider to tend to her needs and accompany her when she is at dinner and in the common areas."

Commentary

Usually the resident will acquiesce and agree to move to health care. Sometimes changes to a resident's living accommodations or routine will be sufficient to allow the resident to remain in independent living. On occasion, the resident or family will arrange for a care provider to assist the resident in the independent home and be a companion in the public areas. In the absence of an agreeable plan, management can ask residents to leave the facility, as they are a danger to themselves or others.

Resident Barriers to the Health Center

While life plan communities provide a continuum of health care, an independent resident is often excluded from receiving a simple medical service unless he or she is admitted into the health center with doctor's orders or the community provides home clinic services. The following narrative illustrates a common occurrence of this.

Gail Shaw was clearly frustrated. She had just returned from the skilled nursing floor. "Henry, they will not rebandage the wound from my fall for me," she said.

"What do you mean? They do that all the time in the nursing area," said Henry. "Our neighbor, Matt , had frequent bandage changes on his burn when he was there."

"They told me that they do not provide nursing services to independent residents," said Gail.

"What is the big deal?...It would only take them fifteen minutes!"

"Now I have to go somewhere else to get it done. I do not have a clue as to who will do it for me."

"This is nonsense. I'm an independent resident, and they treated me after my knee replacement," said Henry.

"Grace Armstrong, the administrator, told me that I need doctor's orders to be checked in," said Gail. "I just do not understand why you were treated after surgery and they cannot replace my bandage."

Commentary

There are distinctions on when and how these medical services are provided. It is important that prospective residents understand and accept the nuances before they move in. Otherwise they will be met with the same frustrations that befell Gail and Henry.

The problem is not with the communities. They would like to provide seamless health care to their residents for all their needs. But they are hampered by state and federal regulations on how and when these services are available. Some services are seamlessly available to all residents, and others are not without a formal transition between the levels of service. Further, there are variations among communities, depending on the government jurisdiction that they are in and the value-added features they offer. This section is intended to explain the regulatory constraints and the choices that communities have in fulfilling their commitment to a continuum of health care.

Skilled nursing, assisted living, and memory care on a community's premises is a sought-after feature among prospective residents. All communities have assisted living and memory care to some extent, and most have skilled nursing on-site. Those that do not will contract the acute care out with a nearby facility. It is natural for new independent residents to assume that these health-care facilities are available to them at any time by just dropping in. This is not the case because independent living, assisted living/memory care, and skilled nursing are governed separately.

In summary, independent resident status in a life plan community implies that the resident is indeed independent regarding his or her health-care needs, not unlike a single-family home occupant.

Health Center Residents Access to Other Facilities

Often residents in these facilities can avail themselves of the many amenities that are available to the independent residents. The specific privileges, of course, may vary among communities. To the extent that they are physically able or have sufficient assistance from others, health-center residents may

+ visit independent residents in their apartments;
+ have their meals in the independent dining rooms or cafes;
+ attend on-site programs;
+ use common facilities, such as the library and fitness center; and
+ have access to the hair salon.

Summary

In this chapter, you have learned about the various health-care services provided to residents and the nuances and regulations associated with providing them. You've been acquainted with the oversight by Medicare of skilled nursing facilities.

Chapter 9

Is It the Right Choice?

Typically, life plan communities' targeted demographic is the upper middle class or wealthier. Entry requires financial resources exceeding a pension and Social Security, with a significant entrance fee, dependent upon the type of entry contract. Most life plan communities are priced at market rate, meaning that all cost is borne by the residents. Entry fees will be in step with the local real-estate market, and monthly fees will be consistent with the local cost of living. Meals, housekeeping, wellness and pool facilities, social programs, health care, transportation, and other services are expensive. Offsetting some of the cost is the ability of residents with type A or B contracts to deduct a portion of their fees from their federal taxes. Some life plan communities may have affordable units if they have generous benefactors or large cash reserves or qualify for local/property tax relief by offering such units.

Most new residents in a life plan community enter independent living. Marketing may emphasize that independent residents can come and go as they please. However, it is not the same independence as a resident has in a single-family home. There are additional codes of conduct that apply in community living. Many are stated in the residence care agreement. Others are implicit, such as civility and respect for others. All rules are for the common good of the community. Residents coming from rental housing, condominiums, or homeowners' associations are aware of the need and take the rules for granted.

Impediments

Moving to a life plan community is a lifestyle change that many are not willing to make. It requires moving from the familiar—your home, neighborhood, and friends—to a community that may be miles away. The apparent structured life of a life plan community may not be appealing, even though independent residents are free to come and go as they choose. Prospective residents may be reluctant to face their mortality by being among others as old as or older than they.

The "Home" Image

Remember the slogan "This is not your father's Oldsmobile" in the late 1980s, when GM gave the Oldsmobile a facelift and tried to sell it to a younger generation? It did not work because under the paint it was still an Oldsmobile.

Unfortunately, life plan communities, as well as most retirement homes, have the same image problem because the uninitiated still envision them as the "Home." Typically, when you mention to your family and friends that you are considering a life plan community retirement home, they have an image of old folks whiling the time away in rockers.

Today's life plan communities are completely different. They provide a wide range of programs and activities to keep their residents alert and engaged. Nevertheless, it is a hard sell. Perhaps the baby boomers will be more open to a retirement lifestyle that is exciting, social, and fulfilling.

Procrastination

Perhaps the greatest challenge to overcome is procrastination. Life is good, you are doing OK living at home, and you're too busy to plan for tomorrow. Then suddenly tragedy or the aging process has caught up with you or your spouse. What to do? The life plan community that you were mildly interested in will not take you. Their mantra is that you must be ambulatory and healthy to enter! You need help now...there is no time to research the numerous health-care centers. Hope for the best! Seniors approaching or in their seventies should not hesitate to consider life plan community living.

Can't Let Go—Really?

home

Many seniors may be reluctant to move into a life plan community, believing their house is a good investment as well as shelter and that costs in a community will be significantly higher than staying in their home. Perhaps this is the case for seniors who are still able-bodied and skilled in doing their own maintenance and upkeep. However, as seniors age, home ownership becomes a burden, leading to either neglect or having to hire out maintenance and upkeep.

Neglect will diminish a home's value, and the cost of maintenance, renovation, taxes, and insurance over the years must be deducted to determine the net gain in value. Further, a senior intending to stay in his or her home should factor in the cost of upgrading the home to

ADA standards should he or she develop mobility problems. An average cost estimate to bring a home up to ADA standards is $39,000.[38]

Generally, home ownership cost for a home without a mortgage will be between 3.5 percent and 5 percent annually, depending on the location and condition. The cost includes maintenance and repair, taxes, insurance, utilities, pest control, lawn service, snow removal, and security. The average cost for a $500,000 home will be approximately $21,250 per year.

The money saved without home ownership will go a long way to covering the monthly maintenance fee associated with a life plan community.

Equally important, selling one's home and moving to a community relieves the resident from the stress and bother of home ownership. Gone also are regular upkeep, liability, disruptive neighbors, and the risk of break-ins and property damage when you are away. Many seniors also have a hard time coping with catastrophic events and emergencies, which are handled by management in a life plan community.

Your Home as an Asset—Is It That Valuable?

Over an extended period, a house will appreciate, but not in a straight line. While there are periods of gain, there are also times of declining value, and sometimes it is extreme, such as during the 2007–2009 crash. The following chart shows a curve comparing the inflation-adjusted housing-price index from 2000 to 2016. Treasuries or investment-grade bonds may perform as well or better.

---

[38] Source: *Remodeling* magazine, 2015.

A Roller Coaster Ride!

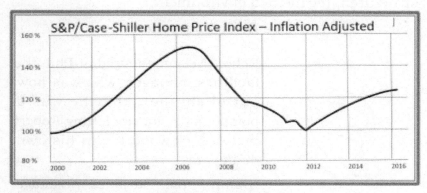

Figure 9.1. Home Index—Inflation Adjusted[39]

Can I Adapt in a Life Plan Community?

The ability to adapt to a structured setting is dependent on one's personality traits and ability to adjust. So, what personalities can adapt, and which cannot or struggle to do so? The answer is not always black and white but often in shades of gray.

My approach in responding to this question is to provide narratives of situations that illustrate personalities who are likely to adapt and others who are not. The individuals and locations in the stories are fictional. However, they represent situations that I have observed during my seven years as a community resident. Each story is followed by my comments. At the end of the stories, I provide a list of Raymond B. Cattell's psychological

[39] Wikipedia, Case–Shiller home price indices, absolute and inflation adjusted, 2000–2016
https://en.wikipedia.org/wiki/Case%E2%80%93Shiller_index
#/media/File:Case_shiller_janv09.jpgex.

factors that are useful in determining adaptability to a structured, regimented environment.

The Do-It-Yourselfer

Robert Nelson shouted at Phil, the facilities manager, who was now out of earshot, that he was a pompous ass for not letting Robert install hardwood tile in his own dining area.

"Damn, the facilities manager stopped me as I was bringing the tile up to our apartment," Rob said to his wife, Evelyn. "It is our apartment, and we should be able to do whatever we like, just as we did in our home over the last forty-five years. I know how to lay tile as well as anybody. Phil tells me that I need to fill out a request for alteration for any changes that we want to have done in our apartment. The request has to include a detailed description of the work to be done and the name of the proposed contractor who will perform the job.

"Further," Rob exclaimed, "before work can begin, they want to verify that the contractor is licensed, bonded, and agrees to perform the installation in accordance with Aloha Heights' specifications. I would not be surprised if they also require unionized workers. Can you imagine how much more this floor is going to cost us without me installing it?"

"You know, I'm sorry that we moved in here," said Evelyn. "I thought tha t we signed up for independent living...meaning that we can do whatever we want when we want. They did not allow me to display our miniature totem pole. And the pink window drapes that I purchased for the living room do not conform to their outside window standard. Since they were custom made, I cannot return them. This infuriates me."

Commentary.

The Nelsons' disappointment is associated with transitioning from a self-sufficient, do-it-yourself experience into a spoon-fed environment with limits on what individuals can do. Most life plan communities will not allow residents to do much more than hang pictures on the wall without permission. Renovations, including painting, must be applied for and approved by management. Work will be done at management's option by either its maintenance crew or an approved contractor.

Most likely, Nelson types will accept the constraints on what they can do. They will soon recognize that the benefits of community living with continuing care outweigh their desire for individual freedom.

The Princess

Mary Clark popped into the hair salon and demanded that Sally, the stylist, touch up her hair next.

"Mary, this is the third time this week that you came in without an appointment," said Sally. "I have other clients who expect to be served at their appointed time. I cannot accommodate you on demand. You need to make appointments that you will keep. Further, you were a no-show on two of the last five appointments that you made."

"My hair needs are not programmed to a calendar," screamed Mary. "I need to be looked after when I have a bad hair day."

Commentary.

The Mary Clark story is about a person who has been pampered all her life. She likely was from a wealthy family with a doting spouse and an extravagant lifestyle. A snap of the fingers usually resulted in instant gratification. Ideally, she should have stayed at home with live-in housekeepers, care providers, and a chauffeur for visits to various events.

How she ended up in a life plan community is anyone's guess. Perhaps her spouse died, or there was a financial misfortune and the community was the best that the family could do. Early-stage dementia is another possibility. Nevertheless, even pampered individuals can adjust to a change in lifestyle when events are beyond their control. Mary did assimilate into the community after a few months.

I'm the Man"

Peter Ray was steaming mad. He had just been chastised for allowing a woman to enter the premises when he left the building abruptly without waiting for the side door to close behind him. The lady was nicely dressed but was a crook. She was found attempting to enter a penthouse apartment when a neighbor became suspicious and challenged her. The neighbor went back into her apartment and called security. By the time security arrived, the "lady" was gone and had successfully burglarized one of the apartments. Building security reviewed the surveillance videos for the outside doors and observed the woman entering as Peter rushed down the street.

Peter has always been a free spirit and in a rush. He ignores all house rules that he doesn't agree with, including the dress code for dinner.

"We're leaving," Peter said to his wife. "I've had enough of the rules here on what you need to do, what you cannot do, how you should appear, and all of the social graces that they expect. You would think that we were in the army...'Yes, sir,' 'No, sir.'"

Liz frowned. She had heard this before, but something in Peter's voice told her that she would not be able to talk him out of it.

"Peter, we cannot leave," said Liz. "We have invested too much time, energy, and money in our decision to move here. It will not be any different at another community or other health-care organization that can look after our future needs. Do you think that we will be welcome at the doorstep of our children in our old age?"

"It doesn't matter," said Peter. "I'm going to tell the administration tomorrow of our intention to move and give them a piece of my mind as well."

Commentary.

The Rays' situation is serious. It is an example of a personality trait that will be difficult to overcome and is at odds with communal living. While Peter Ray's arrogant, competitive, and impatient behavior and disregard for rules may have served him well in his previous life, it is an impediment for peaceful coexistence in a life plan community. Personality traits are ingrained and require diligence and time to change and can be changed only if the individual recognizes the need to change and is willing to devote time and effort. As Liz Ray surmised, they moved out of the community.

Raymond B. Cattell's Psychological Factors[40]

Psychological testing is sometimes used to identify a person's placement in relation to a generally accepted

---

[40] "Cattell's 16 Personality Factors", Kendra Cherry, Very Well, May 21, 2017,

norm or average for human behavior. Psychological tests include an IQ/achievement test, attitude tests, personality test, and others. Of particular interest in my discussion of personality traits that influence one's suitability in a life plan community setting is the personality factor multiple-choice questionnaire by Raymond B. Cattell.

Each of its sixteen factors represents a continuum of human behavior from low to high. An average person would score in the middle. Most would be somewhat close to the middle on either side. There is no right or wrong. However, those who are at the extreme ends will either be praised or cursed depending on the situation and setting. An imbalance of three of Raymond Cattell's sixteen personality factors will make it difficult to live in a community/communal environment. The three factors are:

+ a low range of "Rule Consciousness," such as having a disregard for rules and being self-indulgent and nonconforming;

+ a high range of "Dominance," such as being dominant, forceful, assertive, aggressive, competitive, stubborn, and bossy; and

+ a low range of "Openness to Change," such as an attachment to the familiar, conservative, and respected traditional ideas.

---

http://psychology.about.com/od/trait-theories-personality/a/16-personality-factors.htm_.

7

Cattell developed an assessment based on these 16 personality factors as a Personality Questionnaire.[41] Other personality factors may come into pay if they reinforce the above traits.

Prospective new residents and their spouses should seriously reflect on their adaptability to live in a rule-based community before they commit to moving into a life plan community . If in doubt , they should seek consultation.

Dietary, Environmental, and Lifestyle Issues

Allergies may cause a resident to leave a life plan community. The allergy may be dietary or environmental, such as a neighbor's cat hair, formaldehyde in carpeting, or apartment air that is too dry or too damp. Prospective residents having severe allergies should investigate thoroughly whether a community can accommodate their needs. Do not take the word of marketing. Rather , make arrangements to have a meal or two in their dining room and spend some time in one of their guest rooms. Inquire about air filters, humidifiers, and other items as necessary. Promises made should be in writing to avoid Ruth Jackson's story that follows.

---

[41] Cattell, H.E.P., & Mead, A.D. (2008). The Sixteen Personality Factor Questionnaire (16PF). In G.J. Boyle, G. Matthews, & D.H. Saklofske (Eds), The Sage Handbook of Personality Theory and Assessment: Vol. 2, Personality Measurement and Testing., Los Angeles, CA: Sage.

Unfulfilled Expectations

 Ruth Jackson, a new resident at Oak Manor, was complaining to her dinner companions about not being able to consistently obtain gluten-free meals either at the buffet or from the à la carte menu.

"What is the problem with gluten?" said Ray, a dinner companion. "I'm not sure what it is. I've heard of peanut allergies, but not gluten."

"I have celiac disease and must eat a strictly gluten-free diet, or else I'll get abdominal pain and diarrhea," said Ruth. "Oak Manor is unable or unwilling to accommodate my needs."

"Have you talked to Steve, the dining services manager?"

"Yes, but he tried to evade the question, so I went straight to the chef," said Ruth. "The chef says that he cannot guarantee that any of the meals are entirely gluten-free, because there may be trace amounts in the sauces and condiments and the risk of cross-contamination from sharing the same kitchen platforms and utensils."

"I understand that special diets are routinely provided in the health center ," said Claire, a dinner companion. "Why not i n the independent dining room?"

"I mentioned this to the chef," said Ruth. "His response was that they do special meals when it is in the doctor's orders. In addition, they are not equipped for handling special diets, and the extra cost is not in the fee. He pointed out that he prepares over two hundred meals over a short time. He does not have the resources to prepare special meals."

"So where does that leave you?" asked Ray.

"The chef's closing remarks were for me to use my best judgment and order meals without dressings. When I find something that works, stick with it as long as it remains on the menu. Gee, thanks Mr. Chef, this isn't the gourmet dining that marketing alluded to...I was looking forward to not havin g to cook for the remainder of my life. Further, there is the possibility that we will not be compensated for the meal credits we do not use. And, if we decide to move out, we need to give notice within the next two weeks to obtain a full refund of our entry fee," concluded Ruth.

Commentry

A happy ending! In response to other resident demands, the chef relented and now offers one and occasionally two gluten-free entrées per meal. In addition, Ruth is allowed to take her own condiments and sauces to the dining room.

Nevertheless, Ruth suffered a great deal of anxiety in her fight to take care of herself. When it comes to important matters, verify that your needs can be accommodated before taking the plunge.

As an aside, many life plan communities are now offering gluten-free meals, and some have lactose-free options.

Ruth Jackson's situation emphasizes the need to fully understand the service limitations in independent living in a community. While communities accommodate special diets in their health center, they may not in independent living. Ask marketing for a few complimentary meals in the dining room, and connect with current residents for their observations on the availability of special dietary meals. If there is a resident dining committee, ask for a contact person who may be knowledgeable in how special diets are handled.

Another sensitive area for some residents is the air quality within and around a community. The air may be too dry, humid, or dusty. Those with asthma or other respiratory ailments should ask for an extended free stay to determine their tolerance in the facility. Alternately, they may consider having an air quality inspector test for indoor pollutants. An air quality contractor is available in most metropolitan areas. Their cost is in the range of three hundred to five hundred dollars. That is a significant amount, but much cheaper than moving into a community and having to move out because you cannot stand to live there.

Can I Afford It?

It is not as bad as the saying "If you have to ask the price, you can't afford it." Nevertheless, it is wise to do an analysis on how well your financial resources can withstand the continuing increase in a life plan community's recurring fees as well as the entrance fee.

Entrance fees cover the cost of the independent unit to be occupied and a prorated share of the common facilities. The fee will be similar to a nice home in the area, with adjustments based on the community's location, appeal, and amenities, as well as current economic conditions and competitive market pressures.

Entrance fees are often paid from the sale of the incoming resident's home. Bridge loans can often be obtained if the resident wishes to move in prior to the sale and is reluctant or unable to liquidate other assets.

Typically, a community's annual fee increases match operating cost. For example, the average 2016 increase in California was 3.7 percent.[42] On average, it will be 1 percent or more than the Consumer Price Index (CPI), so don't expect your Social Security check to keep up. As a margin of safety, assume no less than a 4 percent increase in annual fees. Also, consider the incremental increase in monthly fees if or when you or your spouse should move into memory care or long-term skilled nursing. Should you have long-term health-care insurance, it will offset some or all the additional cost.

---

[42] "California Monthly Fee Increases for FYE 2016", CA.Gov, http://www.cdss.ca.gov/Portals/9/CCLD/CCCS/monthlyfees-inc%202016.pdf?ver=2017-07-18-123211-010 .

Table 9.1. How long will you likely live?

Life Expectancy						
Age	Male	Female		Age	Male	Female
Age	Years	Years		Age	Years	Years
65	17.75	20.32		78	9.28	10.86
66	17.03	19.52		79	8.73	10.24
67	16.32	18.73		80	8.2	9.64
68	15.61	17.95		81	7.68	9.05
69	14.92	17.18		82	7.19	8.48
70	14.24	16.43		83	6.72	7.94
71	13.57	15.68		84	6.27	7.42
72	12.92	14.95		85	5.84	6.92
73	12.27	14.23		86	5.43	6.44
74	11.65	13.53		87	5.04	5.99
75	11.03	12.83		88	4.68	5.57
76	10.43	12.16		89	4.34	5.17
77	9.85	11.5		90	4.03	4.8

Consider how long you and your spouse are likely to live following your move-in. Table 9.1 provides average life expectancy. Adjust the averages shown for a margin of safety. About one out of every four sixty-five-year-olds today will live past age ninety, and one out of ten will live past age ninety-five.[43] Do you have sufficient resources for the duration? If in doubt seek the assistance of a financial planner.

When Is It Too Late?

In this section I present the two most common scenarios where prospective life plan community residents waited too long to enter a community. In the first scenario, the prospective residents were denied admission. In the

---

[43] Fig. 1, "Survival Probability for Males, Females & Joint Survivorship," KITCES, https://www.kitces.com/blog/whats-your-longevity-assumption-are-planners-being-too-conservative/ .

second scenario, the residents failed to adapt and assimilate into the community. A third scenario follows the first two as an antidote. It involves a timely move-in.

Denied Entry

"Damn," said Hector to his daughter Nancy. "I got a call from Mountain Crest, and they regrettably informed us that we do not qualify for independent living in their facility because of your mom's early - stage dementia. They did say that when the need arises, they would take Beth in 'memory care ' at market rates."

"Oh, thanks one hell of a lot!" said Nancy. "Where are these guys coming from?"

"Bruce, the marketing guy, gave me this song and dance that they cannot take on the known costly liability associated with an independent-living applicant who will definitely require memory care in the future. He suggested that we try a community that has tiered pricing based on services rendered for each stage of living, be it independent, assisted living, memory care, or acute/skilled nursing."

"You need to be more explicit," said Nancy.

"As I understand it, from an accountant's point of view, the monthly fee for independent living at Mountain Crest includes an accrual of the anticipated costs for future health care for the lifetime of the resident. In doing so, the monthly fee is the same regardless of the resident 's care. The accrual is actuarially based on applicants being in relatively good health when entering independent living. His argument is that Beth doesn't fit their profile of a qualified applicant," said Hector.

Commentary.

All life plan communities provide health care to residents as they age and may progress from independent care to areas of greater need, such as assisted living, memory care, or skilled care. However, they rely on a portion of the independent-living residents' fees to offset their future health-services cost. Thus, they are reluctant to accept a prospective resident who is known to need health services soon.

Too Late to Assimilate

As their airplane was taxiing to the gate, Grace looked worried. " What is troubling you? " asked her husband, David.

"I'm having a haunting feeling that we may not be doing the right thing in convincing Mom and Dad to move into Pacific Heights," said Grace.

"We've been over this a hundred times. Your mom has limited use of her right hand after her stroke, and as near as we can tell, she isn't religiously taking the meds to prevent another one. Dad is being very stoic and is doing all of the housework and cooking, even though he has no skill at it. God only knows how nutritious their meals are. Dad's eyesight is failing , and he will likely fail the eye test when he has to renew his driver's license. Without a car, they will be dependent on Meals on Wheels. They have been isolated in their house so long that they no longer have friends to socialize with or who can help them in a pinch. What a dismal existence!"

"How has it come to this? I remember that their fiftieth anniversary was celebrated with so many of their friends and neighbors."

"Well, while they are joiners, they are not initiators. It was Uncle Ray who orchestrated the anniversary. As friends and neighbors moved and died, they did not compensate by reaching out for new friends and acquaintances. After Barbara had her stroke, she was too self-conscious to get involved. Their world has gradually closed in on them."

"If only my brother, Roger, could be with them more."

"It is not fair to require Roger to be the sole person in their social life. He travels a lot with his job, and his kids are a handful. His wife, Lorena, and Mom will hardly speak to each other after Mom told her how the kids should be raised. Neither we nor your sister, Yvonne, in Alaska can easily respond if there is an emergency."

"Rationally you are right, but they are resisting making this move to Pacific Heights. They are looking at it as an ordeal rather than an opportunity to meet new people and get involved in the programs and activities that are being offered...Oh, here is the gate!"

"Well, let's get on with it. I'll pick up the luggage and meet you at the car rental. Ideally, we will get to their house before noon," said David.

***

"Hello, Mom and Dad," said Grace.

"Oh, we are so glad to see you," said Barbara, Grace's mother, with tears in her eyes. " Give me a hug. I felt so useless in preparing for this move."

While David helped Ted in the kitchen, Grace consoled Barbara regarding her apprehension about moving.

"Am I going to fit in?" said Barbara. "Will people notice that I can't use my right arm or that I scribble when writing with my left hand? We haven't mixed with others in several years. I don't recall how to start a conversation. Are they going to pick on us? What should we be wearing?"

"Mom, you'll do just fine. Other residents in independent living may have similar problems. One thing that they have in common is an affinity for all. It is communal living, and they care for one another."

***

"Hi, Roger, I see that you have things pretty much under control with the movers and the placement of the furniture, " said Grace. " We are planning to have dinner with Mom and Dad here to try to ease their transition. Can you join us?"

"That's an excellent idea. They have been dreading this move and show little enthusiasm for living here. Intellectually, they know that they will be better off, but they don't have their hearts into it," said Roger.

Four Months Later

" Hello, Roger. This is Grace. Every time I ask Mom and Dad how they are doing at Pacific Heights, they are either noncommittal or complain about the old folks among them. Never mind that they are not spring chickens themselves and are above the median age there. When I quiz them on what they are doing during the day, I don't get the sense that they ar e participating in any of the programs that are available at Pacific Heights. What gives?"

"You're right. The y have not assimilated into the community. Their social outlet is their TV. I've considered taking a hammer to it to force them outside of their apartment. At dinnertime they either eat alone in the dining room or more frequently do carry-out and eat in the apartment so that they do not miss a particular TV show. It is no different than when they were living in the house. The best that can be said is that we do not have to worry about their care as their health fails," said Roger.

Commentary.

Ted and Barbara are representative of a few life plan community residents who have not been able to comingle with the other residents. They tend to keep to themselves and eat alone. While their physical health-care needs are being met, they are missing out on the social camaraderie and the multitude of group activities that are available to them. They are paying for these activities but not using them. Unfortunately, they are entrenched in past habits.

Had they considered entering a community when they were still socially active, they would likely have been able to assimilate into the community and have the support of friends. While it is never too early to enter a community, there is surely a risk in waiting too long.

When is the ideal time to enter a community? It is when you can participate in most of the activities and programs that are offered and be active in the community. Many wait until they become frail, when many of the activities and programs are beyond their reach.

A Gift

Roberta, with tears in her eyes, began reading a letter to her husband that they had just received from their daughter.

The letter read: " Dear Mom and Dad, I want to thank you ever so much for the precious gift you have provided to me and brother John. At the time I did not realize its value. In fact, I thought that you were off your rocker when you said that you were moving into Cascade Villa. I was confused and envisioned that you were hiding something from us or were taken in by a con. Why would you sell the house that you and Dad adored and John and I have fond memories of? And then, you hand over the house proceeds as a buy-in fee to Cascade Villa. My vision of you and Dad as the energetic couple organizing block parties and traveling the world vanished. You were moving to an old folks ' home! You were not ready for that. You challenged my own mortality.

"Even though you explained that you would still have your independence and Cascade Villa offered many programs and activities to augment what you could still do on your own, I was skeptical.

"This summer I visited Cousin Debbie when passing through Denver. I heard her story about being the care provider for Aunt Margaret. She was thrown into the role when Uncle Joe died, apparently from extreme exhaustion.

"Aunt Margaret was confused and did not know what to do. She had overt signs of dementia, and Debbie got a crash course in caring for her. Upon becoming Aunt Margaret's legal g uardian, Debbie and her husband, Ed, began the tedious task of finding a suitable place for Margaret. Nursing homes seemed too draconian, but suitable memory-care accommodations were too expensive or had long waiting lists. They settled on a reputable memory-care home within five miles of them, but it too had a waiting list. When asked how long it would take to progress to the top of the list, the director said possibly by spring. In the meantime Debbie had to prepare the house for sale and deal with real-estate people who were like loan sharks.

"Four months later Debbie admitted Aunt Margaret into Saint Vincent memory care...her ordeal over.

"Until talking to Debbie, I never imagined the likelihood and difficulty of being a 'parent of a parent. ' I'm so thankf ul that you and Dad had the foresight to plan ahead. I now understand the role and value of continuing-care communities and your courage in moving into Cascade Villa well before you might need their health services.

"Your move was truly a gift to John and me. Thank you so much,

"Your loving daughter, Joan."

Try Before You Buy

If you are still undecided whether a life plan community is right for you, there are a couple of options for trying a community without a large commitment. Most for-profit and some nonprofit communities provide entry under a rental program, and if you are satisfied, you may convert to a care contract. Many nonprofit communities have a short-term escape clause, probably labeled as "post-occupancy rescission period and refund" in the residence and care agreement signed upon entry. It will allow a new resident to leave within ninety days or so without penalty, that is, you will get back both your nonrefundable as well as your refundable entrance fee.

It is not entirely painful if you decide to leave. You'll have to pay the monthly fees while in residence, the cost of restoring the dwelling to its condition at the time of occupancy, and the moving cost going in and out. Moving costs can be reduced somewhat by moving only the essentials upon entry and moving the remainder later if you decide to stay.

If you decide to leave, be sure to notify management within the rescission period. I'm aware of one new resident who could not adapt and moved back to her previous home without notifying management of her intention, thus jeopardizing her refund.

Summary

In this chapter, we've explored personal impediments against entering a community. Affordability was discussed. You heard a narration where a couple enter too late to assimilate and another denied entry because of declining health. Lastly, there is discussion on assimilating in communities, and personality traits that may not be suitable for living within a community.

Part Three

Selecting a Life Plan Community

At this point you are convinced that moving into a Life Plan community is in your best interest. This section will guide you in finding an appropriate community to match your budget, lifestyle, and health considerations. There is an abundance of information on evaluating communities and in accomplishing the move.

Chapter 10

Preparation for a Selection

A successful move into a life plan community requires forethought and preparation. Are you and your spouse in agreement on making the move? Do you have a list of the essential elements and services a community must provide? What are your location preferences? Put together a checklist of what you need to consider when talking to marketing or visiting a community.

Life plan communities are multifaceted organizations that offer a large variety of services and choices of accommodations. As you investigate and visit communities, you will observe many similarities and differences among them. The ambience, tempo, and lifestyle of communities will vary even though the services offered are similar. A lot depends on the nature of the residents as well as the staff.

Prioritize Your Preferences

Table 10.1 is a representative list that you may consider. Identify the importance of each item on a rated scale, such as one to five, and as you compare communities, grade them on your expectation of them fulfilling each attribute listed. The idea is to be focused on what is most important to you as you visit each site, rather than be distracted by things that are not as meaningful to you.

Table 10.1. Community attributes prioritization list.

Attributes	Im-portance	Score	Value
In proximity of places important to me			
Community amenities			
Neighborhood amenities			
Wellness and recreational programs			
Dining and meal quality			
Educational programs			
Spiritual/religious services			
Lifestyle options			
Near family and friends			
Attractive living accommodations			
Attractive campus			
Access to transportation			
Access to local health-care providers, e.g., doctors			
Continuum of care on-site			
Regional climate			
Regional attractions			
		Total:	

Note: A printable copy is available at http://agingsmartly.org.

Establish Your Price Range

Before you begin your search, determine what you can afford as an entrance fee and recurring monthly fees. Expect monthly fees increases to equal or exceed inflation. Would you like to leave an inheritance to your children? These are difficult questions to quantify. You may need to ask for help from a financial planner.

Establish a comfortable price range for the communities you will consider. You need not fear misjudging and overextending yourself. If you apply for entrance in a community under a contract other than fee-for-service, the community will require disclosure of your finances and will make its own determination of your eligibility for admittance. However, you will be disappointed and waste a lot of time if they deny you. As an additional safeguard in the event you suffer a financial loss or live longer than expected, most communities allow a drawdown of your refundable fee to cover your monthly fees. However, they may treat it as a loan and charge interest.

Costs

The primary costs associated with communities are the entrance fee and monthly fees. As explained in chapter 7, "Life Plan Community Finance: Payment Plans," there are many entrance and monthly fee options among communities. Fee-for-service/rental plans require a down payment of a month's rent or more and monthly fees encompassing the value of the living accommodations, amenities, housekeeping, and personal and health services.

Many communities offer two or more contract options,comprising refundable and/or non-refundle entrance fees with monthly fees. Higher entrance fees are accompanied by a higher portion of the fee being refundable. Considering the time value of money, those entering at a young age or with a long life expectancy, as well as those not intending to leave anything to family, should consider a nonrefundable entrance fee contract. Those older or with health problems should opt for the contracts with a larger refundable percentage even though the entrance fee itself will be large.

The entrance fee will be proportional to the value of the living accommodations selected. The monthly fee covers maintenance of your home, housekeeping, dining, transportation, and amenities. Both the entrance and monthly fee, to a greater or lesser extent, cover the on-site continuum of care. Life-care contracts guarantee continued residency in the community even if the residents are no longer able to pay the monthly service fee through no fault of their own.

If you and your spouse have a significant amount of long-term care insurance, you may not need a life-care contract. Consider instead a fee-for-service or type B, modified contract that covers only part of the cost of on-site health care.

Record Your Lifestyle Expectations and Observations.

For most prospective residents, the lifestyle within a community is the most important criterion when selecting a community. It is also hard to determine without several visits to the facility and discussions with residents. Marketing and sales information may be biased. To comprehend how life will be and how you may fit in, schedule several meals at the communities under serious consideration. If you are out of town, ask to stay in their guest facilities. If possible, plan your visits during the week, when most staff-sponsored and resident activities occur. Weekends are usually slow and not indicative of the normal routine. Attend all the open houses and events that marketing offers. Mingle with residents and ask them what it is like to live there. Try to determine their dislikes as well as their likes.

Remember, if you move in and have misjudged the community's living experience, you'll either must accept it for what it is or lose substantial money and go through a lot of trauma moving out. Note that most community contracts have a short-term escape clause if you are not satisfied. But you will not be reimbursed for your round-trip moving expenses, let alone your loss in self-esteem for having made a bad decision.

Do not be shy in requesting the community to comp you for meals and overnight stays. If marketing balks at accommodating you, indicate that you are seriously considering their facility but need further assurance that it is right for you. If necessary, remind them that the average marketing and refurbishing cost for an empty unit is about $15,000, so your request is inconsequential to their overall cost. If you make a bad choice, it will hurt the community as well as yourself. Be sure to check out the following services and amenities,

Crafts and Recreation.

Residents entering a community are likely to continue their avocations and recreational activities.

+ How well can the community accommodate needs? Most have a library, craft, and card/game rooms.

+ What other amenities are available, such as a tennis court, putting green, woodshop, or garage for car hobbyists?

+ Are there clubs associated with each?

✦ Are equipment and supplies community property rather than individually owned?

✦ Can individuals leave work in progress unattended?

✦ What is the availability of nearby private and public recreational clubs and facilities?

Dining.

Checkout the café or casual offerings as well as the evening dining service.

✦ Is diner gourmet, just a meal, or worse yet, a poor meal?

✦ Are the meals nutritious, with plenty of vegetables and fruits?

✦ How is the presentation, and are there linens with nicely decorated tables?

✦ Does the menu contain a variety of soups, salads, entrees, and desserts?

✦ How often does the menu change?

✦ Are meal ingredients clearly identified?

✦ Are low-salt, low-fat, and glucose-free meals available?

Answers to these questions are subjective and should be viewed in the context of the class of communities that you are considering. If you have dietary restrictions, you need to be particularly inquisitive about whether your diet requirements can be consistently met. Tell the wait staff what allergies you may have and ask what menu selections are OK. If the wait staff does not know, they should check with the kitchen without you having to ask them to do so.

Resident Committees.

Nonprofit and many for-profit communities nurture and fund a residents' association that organizes committees consisting of residents who volunteer their time and talent for the good of the community. The reward for being on these committees is a sense of accomplishment and contribution. The committees are governed by the resident association bylaws. Members generally are volunteers who have an interest in a particular activity. In some cases, residents are actively recruited by other members.

Meetings are generally open to all residents. There are two types of committees: those that arrange entertainment and learning programs, and those that provide oversight and resident input on the administration's services. Typical committees in my community include the following:

+ **Art.** New communities typically start with hotel-like art that is repetitive and mostly bland. The art committee will, over several years, attempt to adorn the common areas with original, quality art conforming to particular themes. The art may be on loan, gifts, or funded through a resident foundation.

+ **Clubs**. Many residents form clubs having their own organizational structure and funding. Typical clubs are dining out, wine tasting, book reviews, choir, bridge, and other games such as poker and mah-jongg.

+ **Communications.** Makes recommendations on how to inform residents on the community's business and events. Their challenge is how best to get the message across to residents who have visual and hearing impairments or do not use computers.

+ **Continuing Education.** This committee facilitates on-site and off-site educational classes and venues for residents. Usually these programs are provided at resident cost because neither the community nor the resident association fund events having limited appeal.

+ **Dining.** Conveys resident satisfaction with the dining experience and makes recommendations on all aspects of the dining program.

+ **Health and Wellness.** Critiques and provides volunteers to the assisted-living, memory-care, and skilled-nursing programs, as well as the fitness and wellness programs for independent living. In some communities Health and Wellness are separate committees.

+ **Library.** Many residents moving into a community bring an extensive collection of books that they would like to share. This committee catalogs incoming books and removes duplicates and books without general appeal. Excess books are sold, donated, or discarded. Committee members set up and maintain a system for lending and returning books.

+ **Marketing.** This committee assists marketing and sales in promoting the community and escorts and dines with prospective residents. Marketing and welcoming may be a single committee.

+ **Programs.** This committee plans and carries out programs for residents. The programs provide entertainment, education, and inspiration. The committee may promote outside programs, movies, festivals, and so on.

+ **Transportation.** Provides a consensus of resident satisfaction and requests transportation changes as needed.

+ **Welcoming**. This committee greets new residents shortly after move-in and helps them assimilate into the community.

+ **Others.** There may be committees for governance, emergency preparedness, finance, environment, and facilities.

Salon.

Vanity does not vanish with age. An on-site hair salon is a must unless there is one within walking distance or on the in-house bus schedule. Are there pedicure, manicure, and massage services as well?

Spirituality.

Many life plan communities began a couple of centuries ago as faith-based programs. Today most nonprofit communities continue to be sponsored and managed by faith-based organizations that offer religious services, with attendance being optional. Most graciously accept nonbelievers and those belonging to different religions. In general, secular and for-profit communities accommodate on-site religious programs that are requested by their residents.

Transportation.

Even though most community residents enter having a car, many will quit driving sometime during their occupancy. So, both public and community-provided transportation are important. All communities provide bus service on a set schedule to selected stores, medical facilities, and entertainment venues. Many also provide car or bus service upon resident request. Private trips must be prearranged. Review the community's bus schedule and car service area to see if the coverage is sufficient for your anticipated needs.

✦ Is the charge for individual car service reasonable for your expected use?

✦ What is the availability of public transportation, and how close are the bus stops?

✦ How frequently do the buses run?

✦ Are taxi, Uber, or Lyft service an affordable option?

The farther a community is from an urban center, the more one will be dependent on the community's in-house transportation.

Wellness and Fitness

These facilities are an integral part of a community's obligations to keep their residents active and healthy.

✦ Is there a fitness center that is adequately equipped with cardiovascular and weight/resistance stations? Is there skilled staff to customize a fitness program for residents?

✦ Is there a pool, and are various aquatic programs offered?

✦ Are there supervised fitness programs, such as tai chi, chair chi, cardio strength, mat/chair yoga, Pilates, line dancing, and outdoor walks?

Accessibility Considerations

By their very nature, life plan communities are handicapped accessible, but some are more so than others. Are all common areas on the flat, or must a resident with a walker or wheelchair use a ramp or elevator? Are ramps available for independent-living cottages? Are the hallways spacious enough not to restrict traffic flow when two handicapped residents are having a hallway conversation? These questions should come into play as you consider a community.

Bringing a Pet?

Many seniors with a dog or cat have no intention of moving without them. Most life plan communities allow pets, but with strict rules governing their control and behavior. There may also be a weight limit.

Communities are concerned about unruly animals tripping, jumping on, or biting residents, some of whom are not agile enough to fend off the animal or will take offense. An injury will likely result in a lawsuit against the owner as well as the community. The concern is more pronounced in communities in urban settings with confined apartment-like independent living units. It is less of a problem in large campus communities with cottages that are spread apart.

Typical pet rules are as follows:

+ Pets are confined to the owner's living space unless on a leash or being carried.

+ There shouldn't be persistent barking or whining.

+ Pets are not allowed where food is being served.

+ Pets are confined to a designated pet area when off leash.

+ Owner must clean up after the pet.

+ Owner has dog liability insurance.

+ Dog has passed socialization training.

Prospective residents bringing a pet into a community need to be aware of the community's pet rules and plan to abide by them; otherwise they will not be well accepted in the community. Dog socialization trainers are available in most localities and will provide a certificate for a pet's accomplishments. It is wise to have the dog trained before moving in.

Create a List of Candidates

Most prospective residents will begin their search in communities that they are familiar with or near one of more of their children. Some will have a destination in mind, such as snowbirds looking for places in the Sunbelt. Those looking for the most affordable, best value, or ultimate amenities and lifestyle should sift through many communities. It is unlikely that place-ment agencies will be helpful because most communities do not pay a finder's fee. Thus, an agency has little incentive to assist.

Communities worth considering will have a website that details their services and provides picture(s) of their community. Some will identify their contracts and fees, but most will require a call to marketing for specifics. Nevertheless, their website will generally be sufficient to decide whether it qualifies as a candidate.

For your convenience, my website at http://agingsmartly.org provides a listing by city and state of life plan communities. Clicking on a community in the listing opens the community's website for your perusal. In addition, the website provides a US map with stick pins identifying the location of communities. Upon activating the map, there will be a clutter of pins, with some overlapping. Scroll and zoom in to an area of interest where cities, towns, and roads are identified and pins are separated. Zooming in further will illustrate a community's individual buildings and campus layout. Then click on a pin, and a dialog box will open with the community's name and address. When you click on the name, it will transfer you to the community's website, describing their attractions. If the website is sparse or vague, their accommodations and services are likely to be as well.

Notify Your Family

After deciding to move to a life plan community, but before visiting any communities, is a good time to notify your family, if you haven't done so already.

Children's reactions may vary greatly, from a sigh of relief that you are arranging your future care, you're too young, or what haven't you been telling us. My own family was surprised and thought that we would be moving into assisted living like their grandparents. They did not realize that life plan communities consist of active seniors engaged in a variety of activities, enabling seniors to thrive and enjoy their twilight years.

Explain your reasoning and how you came to the decision. For many seniors, it is about controlling their own destiny while they are able, rather than being dependent upon others to determine their future care. During the exchange, family members may identify issues that you have not yet thought about.

As you progress in visiting candidate communities, share your observations so the family does not feel left out.

Summary
Having read this chapter and recording your expectations and preferences, you are now ready to have a fruitful conversation with marketing and analyze candidate communities in the context of your lifestyle and needs.

Chapter 11

Community Visits

You need to experience life in the life plan communities that you are considering. No amount of research can substitute for being there. If you know someone living at a community that you are considering, ask for an invite. If not, call marketing for an appointment—rather than dropping in unannounced—so the sales representative can schedule time for a tour and provide uninterrupted attention. You may also consider attending an open house or two.

Discussions with Marketing

A life plan community's promise may overstate reality. You need to discover the difference as best you can before committing to a living unit. The community representative who meets you, shows you around, and explains the offering as a salesperson. Many of the representatives are paid on a commission basis. Their job is to put a pretty face on the product and service being sold. While not purposely concealing a weakness, they may not volunteer them either.

Mature communities are likely to have seasoned and knowledgeable sales personnel who can routinely answer your questions and address concerns. However, that may not be the case for a new community or at a presales office for a community under construction. On our first two visits my wife, Margaret, and I had an experience with a sales representative who went into robot mode when I asked questions she did not know. She would mentally process the questions and repeat the canned statement most closely matching the subject. I resolved the dilemma by asking for a different salesperson. Do not hesitate to do the same.

Planning Your Visits

Communities have a rhythm. Committees, clubs, and other working groups generally meet in the middle of the week. Social and entertainment events are likely in the late afternoon or evening. A community will generally be very quiet on a weekend in the absence of scheduled entertainment or a social event.

On your visit observe resident-to-resident and resident-to-staff interaction. Do residents greet one another and act friendly? Do they move with a purpose? Is the staff helpful, and are residents courteous to them? How do you see yourself fitting in? Take a notepad and jot down your observations. Alternatively, for those who are tech savvy, key in messages to yourself on your phone.

Important Inquiries and Observations

✦ Do the exterior and entry to the premises provide a good first impression and the surrounding area vibrant and well kept?

✦ Is resident parking covered or uncovered? Is there adequate guest parking?

✦ Is the interior inviting, attractive, and well maintained? Does the conciege and staff welcome guest and vendors? Is there reasonable access to the common area from all living quarters?

✦ Is there a wide age distribution among residents? A preponderance of eighty-five and older residents raises two concerns. First, are there sufficient active seniors for a vibrant community with self-initiated activities and a strong resident association with a council, committees, and clubs? Secondly, is there sufficient capacity in the health center to accommodate an impending surge in demand? A significant peak of residents at a younger age may have the same effect, but later.

✦ What are the wellness and fitness facilities like? Do they appear to be used, and are there scheduled, staff-directed instruction and events?

✦ Are evening meals a social event or just a meal?

✦ Do the auditorium(s) have adequate sound systems?

✦ What are the schedules for bus services and availability and cost for personal car service?

✦ Is the surrounding community attractive, with stores and services within walking distance? Are there opportunities to volunteer your time and skills?

✦ What are the major public areas, such as a bistro, café, bar, lounge, library, lobby, and gardens?

Inspections

✦ **Independent Living.** What is the size and layout of independent-living units being offered? Ask to visit units that are available and would meet your needs. Is there good lighting, temperature control, and sound proofing? Are the windows tight, and have Thermopane glass? If still interested, ask for floor layout drawings of available units.

+ **Assisted Living.** Visit the facility and observe the mood of the residents and staff. Peek in on their living accommodations . Be as nosy as possible, and do the smell test.

+ **Skilled Nursing.** Make the same observations as with assisted living. Inquire what procedures they are capable of performing and compare that with the common procedures shown in Table 3.1, SkilledNursing: Procedures.

+ **Memory Care:** Memory -care patients should be separated from assisted-living patients and in a secure area so they cannot wander off. The staff should have training on how to communicate with patients without startling them and yet be in control . Surroundings need to include personal items that are familiar to the patients.

Danger Signals

The following are indicators alerting you to proceed with caution or look elsewhere.

Low Occupancy

Full occupancy for a life plan community is generally considered to be 95 percent or greater. This assumes a 5 percent allowance for the time needed to turn over the living units . Occupancy below 90 percent in a mature community needs an explanation . New communities typically need two or three years to ramp up to full occupancy.

Is the Price Too Good?

During times of economic stress, not-yet-filled new or renovated communities may lower their entrance fee to attract new residents. Sounds good, but only if the community is successful in obtaining full occupancy soon enough to avoid default or a cutback in services. My suggestion to those who are risk-averse is to wait until there is indication that full occupancy is imminent. You may not get the best price, but you will sleep better.

Skilled Nursing Issues

A poor assisted-living experience can be irritating and perhaps uncomfortable, but a poor experience in skilled nursing may compromise your health or put you in danger. So it is important to know the level of care being provided by the life plan communities that you are considering.

As discussed previously in chapter 3 under "CMS Five-Star Rating System," three elements of nursing services are rated for each facility. There is also an overall rating. The ratings for all nursing homes are available at the Medicare.Gov website[44]. Once on the website, set the filter to the right of the results screen to "Within a Continuing Care Retirement Community." You may also set the number of stars for the overall rating that you are willing to consider. Enter city and state or zip code, and you will get results for nursing homes that match the search criteria. Scroll down to view the scores for other communities matching your location selection.

---

[44] Medicare.Gov, https://www.medicare.gov/nursinghomecompare/search.html .

Example of a Nursing-Home Medicare Rating

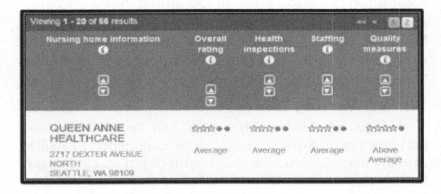

Figure 11.1. Medicare.gov, nursing-home rating

Five stars account for approximately 25 percent of the population , one star for 15 percent , and the three in the middle for about 20 percent each . Avoid communities having only one or two stars for their overall rating.

Also, be wary of communities not providing all the common nursing procedures shown in table 3.1.

Cost Comparisons

It is easy to compare independent living costs among life plan communities . The variables are the non - refundable entrance fee, the time value of the refund-able entrance fee , and the monthly fee . Do this comparison for the two or more of your most likely candidates.

Consider services offered by one of the communities but not at the other . For example , some communities may not allow you to take your own wine to dinner, or they will charge a corkage fee . The cost difference between their wine and your wine can be significant . Some communities do not include housekeeping in their monthly fee.

Also, consider what the incremental cost will be if you or your spouse needs extended care in the health center. This may not be an easy task if you need to com - pare a life-care-plan community against communities with fee-for-service or discounted health services. You not only have to consider the incremental cost difference between the plans but also your risk factor of needing extended care for yourself and your spouse. Your state of health and family history will also come into play.

An approach for comparing communities having different cost coverage for health care is to determine how much long-term care insurance you will need to cover the difference between the two communities. Then add the policy's premium cost to the community with the less coverage and compare it to the cost of the greater plan.

For example, my wife and I were considering two communities where one was a life-care plan covering health-care costs at the independent-living rate and the other plan covered half of the incremental cost for health care. We obtained a price quote for insurance to cover the remaining half of the incremental cost. We added this to the recurring monthly cost of the community providing 50 percent of the health-care cost and then compared it with the recurring cost of the community covering all health care. Surprisingly, the total cost for both plans was nearly identical. I cannot, however, say whether our experience would be typical. Both commu nities were new and offered comparable services and amenities.

You may wish to obtain professional help from an accountant or financial planner in making these cost comparisons.

If you already have long-term care insurance that overlaps that of the community you plan to move into, consider keeping it to offset other costs if your policy is several years old and its premium cost is significantly lower than a new policy.

If you decide to drop your insurance policy, wait until after the post-occupancy rescission period or until you are sure that you've made the right decision on your community selection.

Can You Afford It?

Life plan community independent living fees may appear expensive, maybe even scary. However, they will be partially offset by elimination or reduction of many of your current expenses, such as house maintenance and insurance, transportation, food, gym fees, entertainment , and so on. If you are a budget type of person, prepare a new budget to see what the net change will be between staying where you are versus moving into the community you are considering.

Deposits

At some point , marketing will insist that you register your interest with a refundable down payment to put you on their wait list. It will be a small deposit on the order of a thousand dollars or so that will be partially, if not fully, refundable . Doing so will gain more of their attention , and you may be invited to community events and more meals. Should the wait list grow to a hundred or more or become unmanageable , the community may have a priority wait list with a greater deposit for prospects with significant interest.

Upon selecting a living unit, another deposit will be required to hold the unit. This deposit will likely be ten thousand dollars or greater and fully refundable if you back out. When you make this deposit, be sure to ask for a copy of the residence care agreement. It is an important document that you'll want to review prior to moving in.

Residence and Care Agreement

This agreement is a binding legal contract between you and the community upon moving in. Unless your contract is a simple fee-for-service contract, expect the agreement to cover every likely contingency and be thirty or more pages in length. The agreement identifies the resident's accommodations, benefits, services and continuum of health care. It also identifies the obligations of the resident as well as the provider. Typical clauses may include the following:

+ **Fees:** entrance, monthly, and upgrades
+ **Accommodations** : residence , alterations , utilities, maintenance , guests, pets, and right of entry
+ **Services:** housekeeping, meals, activities, parking, transportation, and extra charges
+ **Health care:** in-home, assisted living, memory care, nursing care, and emergency care
+ **Transfer or change:** of your living unit
+ **Failure to make payments:** termination , financial assistance • Termination: by resident, by management, causation, rescission period, refunds
• **Resident rights, obligations** and rules, handbook

- **Legal:** default, liability,notices, arbitration

If you are unaccustomed to legal contracts have an attorney or financial adviser assist you.

Health-Care Considerations

The pricing models for life plan communities are complex because there are various plans that include an insurance component for the anticipated cost of health care for the duration of residency . Unlike insurance companies that offer long-term care assistance for the essential activities of daily living after a predetermined wait period , most community plans provide immediate short- and long-term health-care coverage for a cost.

Like insurance companies, most communities have a health criterion that future residents need to meet before admission . This criterion is intended to exclude free or reduced-cost health-center service for preexisting conditions that would likely soon require health -center care . Often the applicant may still be admitted but under an exclusion clause stating that he or she would pay for care that is associated with the preexisting condition . For example , a couple moving in with one spouse independent and the other needing memory care would have a cost higher than for a couple with both spouses entering independent , but one needing memory care later.

Summary

This chapter has provided you with information to intelligently inquire and observe which communities will best provide suitable living accommodations, meet your social needs , and offer a continuum of health care.

Chapter 12

Confirming Financial Viability

Once you've made a deposit on a community, you should examine its financials. Do this before your detailed final inspection. Your analysis should be done with the assistance of an accountant or financial planner. I am neither and am not giving financial advice. Rather, the following is an approach that I find helpful.

Gathering Information

The first step in understanding the financial status of a life plan community is to gather the essential information for an informed assessment. Marketing will generally provide financial reports if asked. What can be obtained will differ between nonprofit and for-profit communities because they have different reporting procedures. Privately held for-profits are not obligated to make any disclosure.

Nonprofit Communities

These communities produce monthly financial statements. Ask your sales representative for a current copy. If you cannot obtain a copy from marketing, you may be able to obtain one from a resident council or finance-committee member. The monthly statements are lengthy, with the following information:

+ summary of financial results

- ✦ balance sheet with assets, liabilities, and net position
- ✦ itemized revenue and expense detail
- ✦ operating margins
- ✦ cash flow
- ✦ operating ratios
- ✦ occupancy detail
- ✦ capital assets, i.e., land, buildings, and equipment

Their financials are audited annually at the end of their fiscal period; however, that report is not available until several months later. So, the information will be dated, but is still a good indicator of the community's financial condition.

Ask for their most recent annual report. If not available, ask for a copy of their most recent IRS Form 990. The information on the 990 is extracted from the audited statement, but in a different format. Expect the 990s to be a year old if obtained from the community and possibly two years old from GuideStar.

A community is obligated to provide a 990 to whoever requests one. The penalty for not doing so is a twenty-dollar-per day fine until it is produced. You may also obtain the Form 990 by downloading it from GuideStar if you have either the community's EIN number or the exact name of the community as shown on the 990. Note that the 990 name is unlikely to be the same as on the community's signage and marketing material. GuideStar's website[45] has a search engine for queries

---

[45] "Nonprofit Profile", GuideStar,

https://www.guidestar.org/search#orgStructure .

based on name, location and other factors. Some queries require you to register, such as a search by zip code. However, registration is currently free.

What is important about 990s is the ease in comparing nonprofit communities because data are shown in the same format for all the communities. Also, GuideStar provides a historical view by providing 990s for a three-year period for free and five years with a paid subscription, thus enabling one to see trends in financial performance.

For-Profit Communities

These communities may be under a mix of private or public ownership. Many for-profits are multi-site managed, where the management firm operates the community, but the property may be separately owned and leased to the operator. While you will be able to obtain financial information for the operator, it will reflect all of its operations or its communities, rather than specifically the community you are interested in, unless it has a single-site operator. The for-profit organizations may be a corporation, partnership, or real-estate investment trust (REIT).

As described earlier in chapter 6, "The Circle of Governance," publicly held communities are subject to Security and Exchange Commission (SEC) regulations. They are required to release quarterly and annual financial statements, known as 10-Q and 11-K reports, respectively. Further, they may periodically issue other releases. The earnings releases and summaries are routinely available from investment websites, such as MarketWatch, Morningstar, Zacks, and so on. The 10-Q and 11-K reports can be obtained from the EDGAR.[46]

CARF-CCAC Accreditation

Part of the CARF-CCAC accreditation review includes financial performance. One of their criteria is that a community have a stable financial condition, with no current concern regarding its financial viability. Accreditation also covers other aspects of a community's operation. A description of their accreditation process is availble from from CARF International[47].

Unfortunately, there are only 233 accredited communities[48], a small percentage of the sixteen hundred or so life plan communities. A list of the accredited life plan communities is available from the hyperlink in footnote 47.

Weighing the Financial Risk

In considering a life plan community, its financial condition should be viewed in conjunction with your risk tolerance and the desirability of the facility. A community that is marginal financially but is outstanding in other respects may be worth considering by residents who are not risk adverse. On the other

---

[46] EDGAR is the SEC's Electronic Data Gathering, Analysis, and Retrieval system, https://www.sec.gov/edgar/searchedgar/companysearch.html .

[47] "Accreditations, CARF International, http://carf.org/Accreditation/AccreditationProcess/

[48] "List of CARF-accredited Continuing Care Retirement Communities", CARF International, http://carf.org/ccrcListing.aspx .

hand, couples who are conservative investors and without deep pockets should consider only communities that have passing grades on all financial metrics. This may mean passing over their initial preferences for a more financially stable community.

New communities are often financially vulnerable until they reach full-up status, with a positive cash flow.

Important Financial Indicators and Ratios

As with many businesses, life plan communities have their own unique set of financial indicators that are meaningful in judging a community's financial health. A well-run community will track these indicators on their monthly and annual financial statements. The Commission on Accreditation of Rehabilitation Facilities, Continuing Care Accreditation Commission (CARF-CCAC), ParenteBeard LLC, and Ziegler have developed seventeen ratios for gauging the performance of life plan communities and other rehabilitation facilities. Equally important, CARF-CCAC provides 25 percent, 50 percent, and 75 percent quartile numbers for comparing a community's ratios with its peers. Most communities will report their performance on the following important metrics:

+ **Operating Ratios:** Days cash on hand and debt coverage ratio.

+ **Net Operating Margin Ratio (NOM)** is resident revenue from monthly fees minus resident operating expenses divided by resident revenue. It should be a positive number, perhaps in the 1 percent to 10 percent range.

+ **Net Operating Margin:** This adjusted ratio is similar to NOM, with the addition of net revenue for entrance fees. Expect this value to be 10 percent or greater.

✦ **Operating Ratio (OR)** measures whether cash operating revenues are sufficient to cover the year's cash operating expenses. It is calculated as a percentage, with expenses as the numerator and revenue as the denominator, so the lower the value, the better. A value of 100 percent is break-even. The 2014 median value for accredited single and multi-site life plan communities is 98.5 percent.[49] The year-to-year change can be between 1 percent and 2 percent. Communities with a value over 100 percent have to rely on their entrance-fee income to make up the revenue shortfall.

✦ **Days Cash on Hand (DCH)** is a liquidity ratio. This is a measure of the number of days of cash available for operating expenses from unrestricted cash, cash equivalents, and marketable securities. The 2014 median value
✦ for communities was 311.

Debt Service Coverage Ratio (DSC) identifies the operator's ability to service debt from net cash revenues and net entrance fees. For
✦ communities the 2014 median value was 2.68.

Occupancy, while not a financial ratio, is an important indicator of financial viability. Full occupancy is considered to be 95 percent or above. In normal economic times, community occupancy should not be less than 85 percent,

---

49

Source: 2014 Financial Ratios of CARF-CCAC Accredited Organizations.

and ideally it should be in the nineties, unless you are considering a new community. Lower occupancy needs to be explained to a prospective resident's satisfaction.

Acquiring and Interpreting Financial Data

Values for the above financial metrics can be derived from a community's monthly and annual financial statements. Often the values will have been calculated and printed on the statement. Much can be determined about the financial health of a community from its financial statement.

If marketing is reluctant to furnish you with a financial statement, you may be able to get one from a. resident in a community. Failing this, a nonprofit community is obligated to provide anyone who asks, a copy of their most recent audited financial statement. Recognize that it could be for data up to a year old.

Start your analysis with the cash flow statement. From a financial viability point of view, it is the most important but not the sole criteria. It should show more money coming in than going out. On the financial statement, look for the excess operating revenue, rather than income, over expenses. (The income statement will include noncash items as well). Look at a current month's report as well as the annual report.

Then proceed to the balance and income sheets obtained from the monthly financial statement, audited report, or Form 990. Other key metrics in these reports are the net asset value shown at the bottom of the balance sheet and the net gain/loss from the income sheet.

Financial Comparison between Two Communities

Two-Year Financial Report for a Thirty-Two-Year-Old, Well-Maintained Community

			Prior Year	Current Year
Revenue	8	Contributions and grants (Par	219,461	223,655
	9	Program service revenue (Par	23,701,457	25,643,171
	10	Investment income (Part VII	3,281,625	4,304,653
	11	Other revenue (Part VIII, col	92,463	95,891
	12	Total revenue—add lines 8 th 12)	27,295,006	30,267,370
Expenses	13	Grants and similar amounts p	0	0
	14	Benefits paid to or for membe	0	0
	15	Salaries, other compensation 5–10)	11,342,379	12,516,444
	16a	Professional fundraising fees	0	0
	b	Total fundraising expenses (Part IX,		
	17	Other expenses (Part IX, colt	11,093,040	12,747,818
	18	Total expenses Add lines 13	22,435,419	25,264,262
	19	Revenue less expenses Subt	4,859,587	5,003,108
Net Assets or Fund Balances			Beginning of Current Year	End of Year
	20	Total assets (Part X, line 16)	160,092,978	176,499,230
	21	Total liabilities (Part X, line 2	130,718,977	142,403,860
	22	Net assets or fund balances	29,374,001	34,095,370

Figure 12.1. Form 990 two-year comparison for older community

On its balance sheet, the difference between assets and liabilities is the net asset value , shown as the fund balance . It is $29,374,001 at the beginning of the year and $34,095,370 at year-end, for a $4,721,369 gain. In the for-profit world , the fund balance would be identified as shareholder equity.

Older Community's Five-Year Net Asset Growth

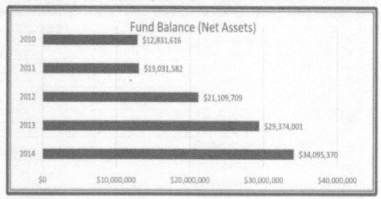

Figure 12.2. Financial comparison for older community
This community 's financial condition exceeds most
value-minded residents' expectations.

Financials for an Eight-Year-Old Community

Opened during the Great Recession
IT'S FIVE YEAR NET ASSET LOSS

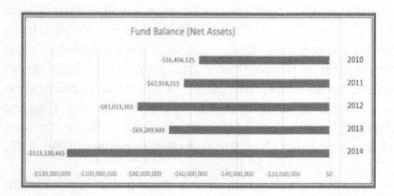

Figure 12 .3. Five -year asset report for newer
community

			Prior Year	Current Year
Revenue	8	Contributions and grants (Part	0	4,354
	9	Program service revenue (Part	24,019,330	22,582,253
	10	Investment income (Part VIII,	86,277	505,577
	11	Other revenue (Part VIII, colu	75,512	74,965
	12	Total revenue—add lines 8 thro 12)	24,181,119	23,167,149
Expenses	13	Grants and similar amounts pa	0	0
	14	Benefits paid to or for members	0	0
	15	Salaries, other compensation, 5–10)	9,396,803	9,874,655
	16a	Professional fundraising fees (I	0	0
	b	Total fundraising expenses (Part IX, c		
	17	Other expenses (Part IX, colur	19,810,624	19,315,108
	18	Total expenses Add lines 13–	29,207,427	29,189,763
	19	Revenue less expenses Subtre	-5,026,308	-6,022,614
Net Assets or Fund Balances			Beginning of Current Year	End of Year
	20	Total assets (Part X, line 16)	239,125,370	233,134,797
	21	Total liabilities (Part X, line 26	308,415,259	346,665,262
	22	Net assets or fund balances S	-69,289,889	-113,530,465

Figure 12.4. Form 990 two-year comparison for newer community

This shows that the fund balance (net assets) gets worse for the eight-year-old community during the year, going from $69,289,889 to $113,530,465, for a $44,240,576 loss. The negative balance sheet is akin to owning a home that costs more than its market value. In this case the cause of the poor performance is slow fill-up due to rough economic times. Digging further into the revenue and expense statements (not shown) reveals that the interest expense of $6,217,171 is 27 percent of revenue.

This is a dismal trend. The good news is that the community has a positive cash flow, shown separately . Their unaudited September 2014 financial report shows a cash gain of $2,875,000 for the year, with a year-end cash and cash equivalents value of $5,890,000.

Although being a risky choice initially, this community received CARF-CCAC accreditation in July 2016, having then reached a stable financial condition as well as providing quality care and services.

Blind Spot

The financial analysis discussed above is based on current and historical data. But what if there is no history to provide meaningful financial data? For a new community, the developer, manager, and bankers rely on a pro forma analysis that may not come to fruition. Typically, the pro forma for new life plan communities assumes that full occupancy will occur in two to three years. If it takes longer or management must cut prices to improve occupancy, serious financial problems are likely to occur. The bankers expect their commitment to be short term and are counting on refinancing and resident entrance fees to reduce the long-term debt. Loan covenants may penalize and tie the hands of the manager and further put the project at risk.

The initial residents are essentially along for the ride. They made their decision based on a sales pitch, a mock-up of the apartments or cottages, and the enthusiasm of moving into a new community. The risk-adverse should wait until a new community is full before making a commitment to move in. If fill-up takes longer than three years, be wary and probe deeply before moving in.

Actuarial Considerations

As mentioned previously, life plan communities offer three types of contracts for future health care. Type A contracts cover all health care at the same fee as independent living. Type B independent resident fees cover part of a resident 's future health care. The remaining cost is billed at the time of service.

Communities essentially insure type A and B residents for all or part of the incurred future cost of their health care. The premium for this coverage is built into the residents 'monthly fees . The actuarial risk is referred to as a future service obligation . As such, it is identified as a liability on the financial statement.

The Accounting Institute of CPAs (AICPA) standard 2014 -0950 requires communities   in 2017 (2018 fiscal) to recognize this cost on their financial statements.

Conclusion

Despite their risks , life plan communities still hold widespread appeal . They promise to alleviate one of the biggest worry facing families with aging loved ones: how to obtain and, in many cases , pay for their future long-term care.

Summary

Here you 've learn   how to acquire   financial information   and evaluate the financial condition of communities under consideration .You now know the distinction between   nonprofit   and for -profit communities financially.

AICPA standard 2014-09 implementing FASB accounting standard ASC—Revenue Recognition.

Chapter 13

Final Inspection

When you reach the point of selecting a community and have made a deposit on a specific living unit, you should do a final inspection and analysis to substantiate your selection. This should be similar to a final inspection that is done when purchasing a house. The inspection should be focused primarily on your independent living unit and the physical characteristics of the facility if you are already satisfied with the community's appearance, amenities, and service offerings from your prior visits. If not, include the inquiries, observations and inspections identified in chapter 12 as well.

   If you have the opportunity, ask a family member or acquaintance who is construction savvy to accompany you. Do not let your escort rush you, and request subsequent answers to questions that cannot be answered during the inspection.

Record Your Inspection

Record your observations and concerns during the inspection so you have a record of deficiencies you may ask management to resolve or take on as tenant improvements.

Table 13.1. Life Plan Community Inspection List

Item	OK	Problem	Resolution
Garage/Parking Area			
Passageways			
Bldg. Integrity & Systems			
Individual Living Unit			
• Interior Layout			
• Windows			
• Heating & Air Conditioning			
• Handicapped Features			
• Interior Construction			
• Electrical outlets			
• Lighting			
• Finishes & Workmanship			
• Appliances & Fixtures			
• Cabinetry & Counters			
• Closets & Storage			
• Housekeeping			
• Internet/Wi-Fi, phone & TV Service			
Write-ins follow			

The above checklist is to assist you during your inspection. A full-page landscape size copy for recording comments is available from my website at http://agingsmartly.org .

If you already decided move into the community, it is still wise to perform the inspection to discover any drawbacks and plan around problems or omissions or emotionally resolve any disappointments before, rather than after, move-in.

For your convenience, the following inspection descriptions are in the same order as the inspection list.

Garage/Parking Area

Urban communities are likely to have garages for resident and guest parking. Suburban and rural communities will likely have off-street parking areas. Outside parking stalls may be covered or uncovered, shared or assigned. Be aware of what specifically would be available to you in the community you are considering.

If parking is in a garage, are you allowed to park the car, or must parking be done by the attendants? If you park, are you assigned a stall, or do you use a shared stall? Either way, is there good lighting and adequate room for you to comfortably park without fear of hitting a post or another car? If valet/attendant parking is used, what are the typical and extreme wait times for retrieving your car?

Can you have a second car? If so, what is the additional recurring fee? How accessible is your car from your living unit? Is there a protected pathway to the car?

Passageways

If you like to mingle with others and intend to frequently participate in social gatherings and events, consider selecting a living unit close to the public areas. If you cherish your privacy consider a more remote unit.

> ✦ **Common area hallways** should be large enough to accommodate dinnertime traffic and

the flow of residents and guests during events. Is there room to pass a person in a wheelchair or walker with a companion by his or her side? Sharp or constricted hallway corners are a potential hazard and may require residents to slow down and proceed with caution. Ideally, common area hallways should be much wider than the hallways to the individual living units. Does the dining room have adequate open space for the free flow of residents and servers during the peak hour?

✦ **Residential hallways** are part of your home and should be well kept and free of clutter. Are the entry doors solid core and tight enough to be an effective sound and fire barrier? Many communities will allow door hangings or provide a small shelf for tasteful personal decorations. However, personal art, decorations, or belongings should not encroach into the hallways, nor should any common area be used as personal storage. Should this occur, it is a sign of weak management, a laissez-faire resident association, and a major concern for a prospective resident.

Building Integrity and Systems

The quality of construction and maintenance of a community's physical plant will greatly affect the recurring cost and livability throughout the facility and especially within your living unit. Generally, the developers and operators of communities recognize the importance of quality construction in lowering the life-cycle cost. However, there can be occasions of oversight or poor design, so consider the possibility of ongoing and future problems.

+ **Mechanical Systems.** If the facility is old, ask if there is a reserve fund especially for replacement of the major systems. Mechanical systems, such as elevators and heating and air conditioning (HVAC), have a useful life of approximately twenty-five years. Electrical and plumbing systems may last a bit longer. A building system may still function but be technically obsolete regarding features and operating cost. Consider the age and condition of the physical plant in the context of your life expectancy.

+ **Environmental risk.** Is the property at risk from natural disasters, such as earthquakes, tornados, and flooding? Is the property up to the current building code, and are there disasters?

+ **Elevators.** If the community has elevators, are they adequate for the demand and sufficiently close to the common areas and all independent living units? Do they appear to be well maintained?.

+ **Trash rooms.** Are trash rooms reasonably close to the independent living units? If appropriate, do the rooms have separate containers for garbage, recycling, and compost disposal? Are the rooms clean and have adequate pickup intervals?

+ **Communications.** Most communities will have an exclusive contract with a local communications providerfor both Internet and

Intranet service. Inquire what services are paid by the community and what are billed to the independent residents.

Individual Living Unit

Be particularly critical about the design, HVAC system, and appointments in the apartment you are considering. The layout of the apartment needs to match your lifestyle and physical condition as much as possible. If you are moving from a large single-family home, any community's apartment will require an attitude adjustment. As metioned earlier, most of your existing furniture may be out of scale for the space available, so plan accordingly. If you are moving from a condominium with equal square footage, you may still have to adjust because of differences in layout. Many community apartments may have larger bedrooms and bathrooms by sacrificing dining room/living room space.

Recognize that few if any of the individual living units in life plan communities will be perfect in all aspects. Judge them on a livability scale with your current arrangement and other choices.

Layout

Because of the scarcity of suitable land, urban community apartments are small or expensive in comparison to their country cousins. You may wish to select a more efficient apartment rather than one that is attractive but has an inefficient layout. Open floor plans are more efficient and can accommodate more or larger furniture than closed plans. Hallways reduce the useful space. Rooms with diagonal or round walls, while attractive, are the least efficient. Custom-made furniture can mitigate problems with irregularly shaped rooms. If you and your spouse prefer separate working spaces during the day, select an apartment with a den or two bedrooms, where one or both are large enough to accommodate daytime needs.

To determine how your furniture will fit, ask for a scaled drawing of a unit that you are considering. When back home, make paper cutouts of your furniture at the same scale as the drawing of the rooms and see how they fit. This will enable you to determine what pieces you may need to replace before you move rather than after. Pay attention to required clearances for movement around furniture.

Windows

The construction and thermal characteristics of the windows are critical to your comfort. They should be triple glazed in locations with extreme winter temperature and double glazed elsewhere. Windows filled with argon gas will also reduce thermal conductivity. The construction and material of the window frame is also important. The window frame should be rigid, fit tightly when closed, and covered with an insulating coating. A bare metal frame will transmit significant heat regardless of the type of glass used. Inspect the gasket between the window and outer frame. Are there any gaps or tears? Evaluate how well the windows block outside noise when shut.

Are the windows appropriately tinted for the local climate and direction they are facing? If not, plan on in-stalling inside shades to compensate. Pay attention to the direction that the windows are hinged. It may limit your choices on window coverings and furniture place-ment.

Heating and Air Conditioning

These systems may be central to all apartments in the building or individual to each apartment. There are pros and cons to each system; however, individual temperature control for your apartment is essential. From the control, turn up the temperature and evaluate how the system responds. If heat and cooling are delivered through air vents, compare the air flow in each room. Does the flow rate appear equal or adequate for the size of the rooms? If not, can the venting for each room be individually adjusted? Overall, does the air appear too strong and uncomfortable? If so, ask if maintenance can adjust it to a more comfortable level. Perform the same experiment with cooling by setting the temperature lower. Determine the top and bottom temperature limits allowed from the control. Is the range consistent with what you would like for both day and nighttime temperature control? If not, ask if maintenance can adjust the range for you. There may be valid performance or maintenance reasons why they cannot. Inquire on how heated or cooled air is circulated within the apartment and whether it is mixed with hallway or outside air. If you have concerns, review the design with an HVAC professional to understand its benefits and limitations.

The adequacy of the HVAC system cannot be completely determined from a single inspection, so ask current residents about their experiences and satisfaction with the systems.

Handicapped Features

Is the apartment laid out and equipped so it can accommodate wheelchairs and walkers with little or no modification? If so, a mobility-impaired resident may be able to continue living independently rather than moving to assisted living. If impairment is permanent, cabinets and counters can be modified or replaced to accommodate a handicapped person, but repositioning walls and changing plumbing will be prohibitively expensive, if not impossible, in multistory buildings. Reasonable accommodation for wheelchairs requires entry and interior doors to have at least thirty-two-inch openings and preferably thirty-six. In addition, there needs to be ample clearance on each side of the door for turning around a corner. The bathroom(s) need to be wide and deep enough to facilitate transfer from a wheelchair to the toilet and bathtub or shower.

Interior Construction

Verify that walls between adjacent living units and the hallway meet code as "party walls." Specifically, do the partitions between dwellings meet HUD's Sound Transmission Class (STC) and Impact Transmission Class (ITC) ratings equal to or greater than HUD's Grade II or preferably Grade I guidelines?[51] Also does the management require all floors above bedrooms and living and dining rooms to be carpeted or else constructed with floating wood or stone with acoustical underlayment?

Is the entry door(s) solid core and tight fitting? Can you hear any sound or conversation coming from the hallway and adjacent apartments? Can you detect cooking odors in the hallways? If so, inquire whether it is a persistent problem.

---

[51] IMPACTA, HUD Guidelines, Codes & Standards for Dwelling Partitions, http://www.soundseal.com/pdfs/HUD%20Guidelines.pdf .

Electrical Service

Are there ample electrical outlets throughout, and are they placed where needed? If allowed and you are comfortable doing it, open the circuit breaker panel and note the circuit amperage allocated to each location. Does it seem reasonable for the load that you expect to use? If the community allows you to have an electric barbeque on the balcony or patio, does it have a dedicated 30-amp circuit? If not, leave your barbeque behind.

Lighting

Is there ample lighting in the kitchen and bathrooms? Are there overhead light fixtures in the bedrooms and den? If there is an overhead fixture in the dining area, is it above the location for a table?

Finishes and Workmanship

Are the walls plumb and floors level? Do the interior doors close tightly and pocket doors move freely? It is a plus if the bedroom and bathroom doors are solid core. Are the wall finishes attractive and durable?

Appliances, Fixtures, Cabinetry, and Counters

Are the grade and condition of appliances, fixtures, cabinetry, and counters consistent with what you expect? If not, can they be exchanged for an upgraded item, and at what cost? If you upgrade, will the community provide ongoing maintenance?

Closets and Storage

As we all know, there is never enough storage space. With few exceptions, this is particularly true in community living. Aside from the closet and cabinet space in the apartment, you will likely be provided with a locker in the basement that is three feet wide, four feet deep, and seven or eight feet high. If it does not have shelving, ask if you can install some. If you move in, it will be a great opportunity to try out the residents' woodshop if one is available. Many residents replace the apartment's original closet shelving with more efficient or attractive closet systems. The lack of individual storage is somewhat offset by the availability of furnishings, equipment, and material in the community's crafts and recreation rooms.

Housekeeping

Many communities provide housekeeping within the resident's living unit. Inquire on the time spent and frequency of service. What is included routinely and periodically? Is there an opportunity to schedule additional services, such as upholstery cleaning? What is the fee schedule?

Internet and Television Service

Most likely a community will contract cable TV and Internet service with a single provider. Often basic TV is included in the community's monthly fee. Residents may have to subscribe with the provider for premium TV and Internet service. Ask for a fee schedule and list of available channels.

Commentary

Few communities are going to score high on all of above items. Consider what your essential requirements are and what is tolerable or fixable within budget. Should you decide to age in your current setting, create contingency plans for health-care service should you need them.

Summary

This chapter has provided you with inspection criteria for substantiating your choice in a community before paying your entrance fee. It also enables you to prepare a list of items you feel should be fixed prior to move-in and plan modifications that you will be making.

Part Four

Making the Move

Unless thoughtfully planned and executed, a move can be a gut-wrenching experience. This section is a guide on accomplishing the process from selling your house to taking delivery of your furnishings at the Life Plan Community.

Chapter 14

Moving Arrangements

Having made a decision to move into a specific life-plan community, a feeling of excitement, anticipation, and perhaps anxiety may flood over you. Moving is a daunting task. This chapter identifies the resources, activities, and coordination needed for a successful move.

Selling Your Home

This will likely be the most difficult part of preparing for your move. If it is the house in which you raised your children, you will have fond memories, and it may be tough to let go. Further, your perception of its livability may be very different from that of prospective buyers. Over time, styles and consumer demands change. You may have to make modifications to your home to be competitive and have it sell in a reasonable time. Your real-estate agent can advise you on changes that will make a difference and will provide a return on your investment. For example, homes with open floor plans are more desirable than older layouts, with living room/dining rooms separated from the kitchen. Before we sold our condominium, we replaced the wall between the kitchen and the living room with a half wall at a modest cost so the kitchen was open to guests seated in the living room. Our only regret was not having done it earlier.

Real Estate Market Influence

If you are lucky, a hot real estate market is an ideal time to sell, particularly if you live in a desirable location.

Prospective buyers will overlook a lot of warts that in normal times are showstoppers or items that they will haggle on. In hot markets, good homes will have offers before the first open house.

The exact opposite happens in a weak market, such as during the great recession. Then, a house needs to stand out to even get an offer.

Things to Improve Value and Salability

+ **Make it sparkle** and ready to move in with no deferred maintenance. Carpets and floors should be in good shape, windows clean, paint fresh, and the landscaping should be attractive.

+ **Be realistic in pricing** your home. The market rather than your expectations governs the selling price. In a fluid market, you may need to adjust your pricing and expectations accordingly. Case-Shiller produces a housing price index for twenty metropolitan areas, with a national and composite index for the twenty cities. From the Case-Shiller index[52] for the area nearest your home, you will be able to observe price trends and adjust your price and expectations accordingly. The index lags actual selling prices by two months and is reported monthly. The index can be found from the hyperlink in footnote 51.

---

[52] "Table 2, Case-Shiller Indices for 20 Metropolitan Areas", S&P Dow Jones Indices, https://www.spice-indices.com/idpfiles/spice-assets/resources/public/documents/557549_cshomeprice-release-0725.pdf?force_download=true .

+ **Consider professional staging**. Admittedly, this is costly, but it will add attractive furnishings and wall hangings to complement the house and match the taste of targeted buyers. Often, dated furniture will be substituted with contemporary furniture. A good stager will make the house appear larger than it is. During the height of the great recession, we staged our condominium eight months after we had listed it without receiving a single offer. We sold it six weeks after staging.

Financing your Entrance Fee

Most new community residents use the proceeds from the sale of their home to cover their entrance fee. However, if you cannot or do not wish to sell your home before moving in, there are possibilities for temporary financing other than selling investment assets. Opportunities for raising the necessary cash without liquidating assets such as stocks, bonds, and real estate follow. Because of their complexity, please consult with your financial adviser before using any of them. I am neither a tax nor financial advisor.

+ **Obtain a bridge loan.** This is the most likely approach if you need to borrow a significant portion or the whole amount of the entrance fee. Your ability to acquire a loan, as well as the interest rate and fees, will be governed by your credit rating, net worth, and negotiating skills. Start with the banks or credit union that you currently do business with. Also, ask the community if they have a standing arrangement with a bank for the purposes of assisting new buyers in covering the entrance fee. Expect to pay a loan fee as well as interest. You may also have to pay an appraisal fee if your house is the collateral for the loan.

✦ **Borrow from your life insurance**. You can borrow against a whole life policy up to the amount of the surrender or loan value. No repayment is required when you borrow from life insurance. However, you will incur interest and possible fee charges.

✦ **Borrow from your Roth IRA**. You can only borrow from a Roth IRA as much as you contributed in the current calendar year, but you must return it prior to April 15 of the next year. The amount that you can borrow will likely be insufficient for your needs. Alternately, you can withdraw as much as you like from your Roth IRA if you are age fifty-nine and a half or older. Once the money is withdrawn, you cannot return it, and you lose the advantage of tax-free growth in your Roth account.

✦ **Pull cash from your brokerage account**. Many investors have a margin account even though they do not buy on margin. Margin accounts are needed when a client sells a stock short or borrows to buy. If you have such an account, you can borrow against it up to its value less the margin maintenance amount. There is generally no fee, and the interest rate will typically be similar to that of a bridge loan.

✦ **Borrow from your 401k plan**. This is an attractive alternative, provided you are sure you can repay the loan within one year. Otherwise, it is considered a withdrawal and is taxable. The amount that you can borrow is the lesser of $50,000 or 50 percent of the account balance.

+ **Borrow from your traditional IRA.** You cannot borrow per se; but you can transfer money from one IRA to another or a new account. You have sixty-days to complete the transactions without penalty. However, if you miss the deadline, the full amount that you withdrew is taxable. Ouch!

Already Have Long-Term Care Insurance?

Those having long-term care insurance should determine whether it is better to maintain their policy and sign up for a community plan that covers partial or no health-care coverage or to drop their insurance policy and opt for a community life-care plan. If you've had your insurance policy for a long time, it may be cheaper to maintain your policy. If you do, be sure that your future health care in the specific community you chose is covered by your policy and whether payment is made to you or directly to the community. It is best to make this determination beforehand by meeting with your insurance agent and community representative, as well as reading the fine print in both the insurance policy and residence care agreement. If you decide to drop your insurance policy, wait until after the post-occupancy rescission period or until you are sure that you've made the right decision on your community selection.

Plan Well before Moving

A successful move is much more complicated than simply calling a full-service mover who will pack your furnishings and deliver them to your new home.

Determine What to Take

You will need to pack lightly if the space you are moving into is smaller than where you currently live. It is best to dispose of items that you will not need or cannot use before your move. Otherwise, you will clutter your new home with items you should not have packed. The steps that you need to go through for a successful relocation follow.

✦ **Furniture.** If you have not already acquired a large-scale drawing of the apartment or cottage that you will be moving into, ask for one. Make sure that it shows the location of electrical and TV outlets and how doors swing when opening. Using paper cutouts for your furniture pieces, decide what to take and their placement. Be aware that if you are moving from a spacious home, much of your furniture may be out of scale for your new living quarters, particularly if you have been fond of country and overstuffed furniture. Now is the time to treat yourself to new furniture. Consider European style that is chic and fits nicely in smaller spaces.

Even if your community apartment has the same square footage as your home, you may be surprised to find that not all your furniture will fit well. My wife and I personally experienced this problem. The condominium that we moved from had larger common rooms and smaller bedrooms and bathrooms. Consequently, we had to buy new living room furniture. Typically, community apartments' baths and bedrooms are larger to accommodate walkers and wheelchairs, if needed. The common areas shrink because of the diminished need for entertaining a large group.

Allow yourself enough time to dispose of the furniture you will not be taking and arrange for replacement furniture to be delivered concurrent with or closely following your move-in.

+ **Kitchen and Household Items**. Even though you will be moving in as an independent resident, you may consider reducing the amount of kitchen and household items you bring along. Community apartment kitchens are generally sparse and insufficient for preparation of full meals for many guests. Most independent residents will entertain guests in one of the community's dining rooms rather than preparing a big meal in their apartment.

Communities may provide housekeeping service and perform all repairs, so most items that you have for upkeep of your home will no longer be needed.

+ **Clothing.** Compare the amount of hanger and drawer space you currently have with that at your new home and adjust what you will take accordingly. Alternately consider installing a closet system that will provide greater utilization of space.

Dispose of Items No Longer Needed

Begin by segregating items into groups consisting of:

+ **Items for family and friends.** Ask recipients to pick them up before you move.

+ **Sentimental items.** There may be a child or other family member who has coveted these items and would love to keep them in the family.

Items to sell.

+ **Use the Internet** to determine fair value for recent or common items. For example, eBay or Craigslist will identify pricing for identical or similar items. If you use eBay, click on advanced search and then on "sold items" under "Search including" for an indication as to what the item is selling for rather than what it is priced at. It is more convenient to sell through Craigslist because the buyer comes to you and pays cash. You may get more on eBay, but you must arrange shipping. You may also have to take it back if the buyer is not satisfied.

+ **Consider consignment stores** for vintage clothing, accessories, fine furniture, and jewelry. Consignment stores often specialize and may refer you to an appropriate store if they are not interested in an item. If you have something too heavy or bulky to carry, show them a colored picture to see if they are interested. Depending upon the item, a store will pay the owner 40 to 50 percent of the sale price and return the item if it does not sell within a prescribed time.

- ✦ **Auction houses.** Many auction houses have weekly or monthly auctions for antiques, collectibles, original artwork, and furnishings.
- ✦ **Silver and gold pieces.** Sterling silver and gold ware are often worth more for meltdown than resale value. You can get instant cash when selling them for meltdown.
- ✦ **Garage or yard sale.** You need to be well organized and have a bit of luck to have a successful yard sale. It takes a lot of work, and often you will still have to dispose of unsold items. Do you have a covered space if it rains? Is there sufficient table space to attractively display higher-value items? Often the revenue from a sale is not worth the effort.
- ✦ **Donate.** Usable clothing, furnishings, crafts, CDs, tools, and toys can be donated to various charities, such as Goodwill, Saint Vincent de Paul, and so on. Do not donate stained or damaged articles. Clothing should be washed or cleaned before donating. Unfortunately, books no longer have much value, and many places will not accept them.
- ✦ **Discard** the remainder by either recycling or tossing in the garbage.

Tenant Improvements

Most likely you will want to make changes to the interior of the living unit you will be occupying. It may be cosmetic, such as changing the wall color or light fixtures. Consider hiring an interior designer if you are not comfortable doing your own design and selecting the appropriate pieces. Functional changes may include adding built-in cabinets or replacing the appliances or closet system to match your needs or taste.

For example, when Margaret and I moved into Mirabella Seattle, we added a built-in shelving unit below the lip of the kitchen counter that was initially intended for stool seating. A sewing center was installed across the full length of one of the bedrooms, closet shelving was added, the bedroom hollow-core doors were replaced with solid-core doors, and most lighting fixtures were changed. We also added a sunscreen on the patio.

Plan your improvements and order long-lead items before your move-in date. If the unit is unoccupied, you may be able to have some or all the changes accomplished beforehand. Work closely with the community's move-in coordinator, as they must approve changes and authorize the contractors doing the work.

Unless a community provides an allowance for tenant improvements, expect to pay for your improvements and their maintenance during your residency.

Upon vacating your living unit, you or your heirs may be responsible for removal of your improvements. It will depend upon what is said in the residence care agreement and whether the new tenant wishes to keep them.

Arranging the Move

Select a moving company weeks before the move but after you have decided what furniture to keep. Moving a household is complex and should not be left to chance. Be informed of the options offered by moving companies.

+ **Selecting a Moving Company.** Obtain recommendations from neighbors, friends, and family who have hired a mover recently. Ask for and check the company's references and inquire about the company's consumer complaint history at the Better Business Bureau. Be wary of a bureau's rating for the company because it may not be entirely objective. Bureau members may unduly influence their rating. Trust your instincts: if a mover makes you feel uncomfortable, go with another company.

+ **The Moving Cost.** Your utilities and transportation commission sets the rates that a mover can charge. Moving costs are calculated by one of two methods. Short-haul moves are typically within a metropolitan area. Their rates are based on the workers' hours times an hourly rate for loading, moving, and unloading your goods. Long-haul and interstate rates are based on the weight of your goods and the distance hauled. Extra services offered by moving companies include the following:

1. Packing/unpacking.
2. Disconnecting and reconnecting appliances (washer, dryer, icemaker, and so on).
3. Boxes and packing materials. (Tip: You may be able to get leftover boxes from the community or on Craigslist.)
4. Shuttle services between the truck and the residence, when needed.

+ **Lost and Damaged Goods.** Movers have some level of liability for loss or damage to your belongings during your move, but their liability will likely be less than the value of your goods.

The mover is not liable for the full value of your property unless you pay an additional charge for the protection. Obtain specific descriptions of the protection plan that they offer. Note that homeowner's insurance policies do not cover moving.

Packing the Goods

You may choose to pack some or all boxes yourself. However, movers are not liable for damage unless there is damage to the container and inspection is done at the time of delivery. If you pack yourself, do as much as possible before the moving day. Label all boxes with their contents and destination location. Colored tags are a good way to identify rooms items need to go to. You or the mover should maintain an inventory of what is being moved.

Arranging Delivery

The life plan community will have a move coordinator who will instruct the mover where to park and the pathway for delivery to the resident's apartment/cottage. In a multistory building, the movers most likely will be directed to a freight elevator that will be dedicated for their use.

Be on-site during delivery to instruct the movers where things go. If you are not there, have someone you trust represent you. Check for damage, particularly to valuable items, while the mover is present. You or your spouse should be there when boxes are unpacked so you can control where the furnishings go.

If It's Too Complicated

Moving, well, takes a lot of time and energy. Rather than do it yourself, consider hiring a moving coordinator, who will do the packing, unpacking, and coordination with the moving company and community. Do you really need the grief of doing all of this yourself? A coordinator may save you money if you mess up the move or ship furnishings you cannot use.

Summary

Making the move into a Life Plan Community is similar to moving from a house you own or rent to another.

In this chapter, you have received tips on selling your home, financing your entry into the community, disposing of possessions that you will not need, arranging the move, and taking delivery of furnishings. You've read about tenant improvements and tradeoffs between various contracts and long-term care insurance.

Chapter 15

Your New Home

This chapter is a guide on the nuances of living in a life plan community. It identifies information sources for settling in, help on meeting your neighbors, and the importance of looking forward to and getting into a routine.

Hesitant Anticipation

Buzz! Buzz! Buzz! "Get the door," Ken said to Alice. "It's the movers."

"Good morning, madam, I'm Maurice...Jake and Trevor will be assisting me in moving the remaining furniture to Beacon Heights." Alice was amazed at Maurice's build. He was big and muscular, yet he had a personable and "in command" disposition. Our furniture will be in good hands, Alice thought. She smiled, thinking about her daughter-in-law, Barbara, who had arranged the move and convinced them to acquire some new furniture that was in scale with the room sizes at Beacon Heights.

"Barbara will have the previous load unpacked and neatly placed in appropriate locations when we arrive," said Ken.

As the movers were leaving, Alice looked around and was saddened. "Oh God !" Alice exclaimed, "I'm going to miss this house, the garden, and neighborhood. I remember the neighborhood parties, the big dinners that we hosted, and the kids ' swimming meets at the club."

"Yeah," said Ken, "but how many of the old gang is still here? And of those that are, would any still be here for us if we needed help? The garden has gone to seed, and it has been a year since our last big dinner party. When we need to entertain a large group, Beacon Heights has a lovely private dining room where we can have a meal catered. For your memories, I've scanned all of the pictures we have taken here and downloaded them onto the digital picture frame that will go on your desk."

He is right, thought Alice. Of the furniture and articles being left behind, most are dated, well worn, and too large or inappropriate for our new home. "It is stil l the home that I've known for the last forty - five years," lamented Alice.

Alice's mind wandered over the events that led them to decide to move into a life plan community and Beacon Heights in particular. An accumulation of things became convincing, like rattling around in a multistory house that required time-consuming upkeep and maintanence and was far larger than they needed. Ken would sooner be golfing than cutting the lawn. When traveling, they had to always make arrangements to have someone look after the house. Alice recalled the trip when the house was burglarized and she felt violated for over a year. They still wanted to continue traveling and have an active lifestyle, but without being encumbered.

Ken and Alice decided that they needed a safety net that would provide a continuum of health services should they need it. Further, they wanted the services to be available on the premises where they lived. This really struck home last year when Alice was diagnosed with beginning earlier stage macular degeneration. Sure, modern medicine could forestall but not prevent its progression.

"I'm glad we are moving into Beacon Heights," said Alice. "I'd be trapped living in the suburbs if I los e my driver's license."

"It will be a new experience for us to use bus service for shopping, errands, and getting to cultural and sporting venues," said Ken. " Further, Beacon Heights' s car service is available on a prearranged basis. No more forty-five-minute treks to get to the opera and symphony. Look, Saint Mark's Cathedral is to the left...we should try it out."

As they reached the entrance to Beacon Heights, Alice exclaimed, "Can we adjust?"

Settling In

In many respects moving into a life plan community is an adventure unlike anything you may have experienced before. It is communal living with a large support group of like-minded residents? Initially it can be daunting because of the difference from what you are used to. However, if you ask, the administration and fellow residents will offer assistance and guidance.

Unpacking

Residents moving in will most likely be assigned a storage locker for items they may need periodically but do not want in their living area. Ideally, there will be a place for everything you have taken. If you misjudge, it is best to remove the items to avoid clutter that may put you at risk of falling.

Unless you have planned very well or have a lot of help, it may take a few days to settle in. In addition to unpacking, there may be some rearranging, pictures to hang, and perhaps new window coverings to install. If you are overwhelmed, you can ask the community's moving coordinator to arrange for maintenance workers to assist with placement of furniture, installing shelving, hanging pictures, and so on.

Welcoming Committee

Communities may have a welcoming committee to greet and assist new residents in settling in. Committee members will introduce new residents to current residents who may have a similar interest or background. A committy, in conjunction with administration, may host an orientation where staff and resident organizations can explain their roles. Working with marketing, some committees may host prospective residents, so should they move in, they will already be acquainted with the community.

Inform Visiting Family and Friends

Communities are closed to the public. Entry is by invitation, especially in the common areas. The health center is required by law to be secure. If a community's independent living areas are in the same building as the health center, entry into any part of the building is controlled. Guests enter through a lobby where the receptionist verifies that they are invited and will issue them a badge to wear during their visit. Multiacre campus communities may have a drive-through gate at the entrance of the complex.

Often residents can arrange for family and frequent visitors to be issued permanent badges for their entry.

Getting into a Routine

Take time out to meet your neighbors, accept some help, and attend programs and social events as they occur. Gravitate to groups of common interest—for example, knitting, painting, writing, sewing, woodworking, or volunteering. If you do not know anyone when you move in, ask the dining receptionist to seat you with other residents. Without exception, current residents will greet you warmly.

Look over committee and group organizations to find ones that you might like to join. You can attend a meeting or discussion without obligation.

Think like a Renter

New residents, coming from a home that they've maintained over many years, should readjust their thinking regarding home repair. Except for improvements you have made or arranged on entry, all other maintenance problems and repairs are the responsibility of the community's maintenance personnel. Housekeeping service is likely provided.

Information Overload?

Life plan communities are complex given their size and the abundance of services that they provide. In addition to the residence care agreement, which should be stored in a safe place, you will receive the following publications and be informed of the communities' Intranet information. Initially, the move-in guide is what you need. If there isn't one, then refer to the resident handbook.

✦ **Move-In Guide.** This document will be somewhat redundant to the resident handbook, but much more specific on how to contact staff, how physical things work, and how to get things done.

✦ **Resident Handbook.** This will likely be a twenty-plus-page document identifying all the services and amenities offered and how to obtain them. There will be information on dining and meal takeout and hours and dress code for the various dining areas. It will have resident association information on committees and clubs. The handbook most likely will be a governing document referenced in your residence and care agreement and may be amended from time to time.

✦ **Forms and Notices.** Notices of upcoming events will be displayed discreetly and often distributed in your community mailbox. Forms for ordering services and making modifications to your living quarters are readily available.

✦ **Intranet.** Many communities have their own Intranet that can be read by any web browser and most smartphones. The technical word for it is content management system (CMS). It is an online depository for everything that is published in the community. It will be easy to search, with tabs for calendars, directories, dining, departments, services, and resident groups. You can then inquire into subheadings. Past publications are archived; for instance, you may be able to obtain the minutes for an art committee meeting years ago. An example of a community's activities is shown in Figure 4.3 Life Plan Community's Intranet.

+ **Community TV Channel.** Many communities arrange with their cable TV provider for a channel that can have a rolling display of upcoming events and notices. This is particularly useful for residents who are not computer literate.

+ **Community Periodical.** As described earlier most communities publish a newsletter or periodical on happenings within the community, scheduled events, administration announcements, and resident stories.

+ **Telephone Service.** New residents might think that they must order a telephone line as soon as they enter a community, or they may decide that their cell phones will be good enough. They will be surprised to find that in most cases phone service is included. If so, the community will provide phone service through a dedicated private branch exchange (PBX); such a system is normally used by businesses. Call connections among the residents and community's staff are made within the PBX rather than being switched through at the phone company's central office. A resident's phone number will still be seven digits. The first three will be common to the community, and the last four digits direct the calls to each living unit and staff members. To connect with someone internally, you just dial the four-number extension. Outside callers will be able to reach you directly by dialing all seven digits, the three for the community followed by your four-digit extension.

✦ **Long-distance charges** will be handled either by the community billing you directly or by being absorbed as an expense by the community. Today, long-distance calling is so inexpensive that the cost for a community to bill a call may exceed the cost of the call.

Emergency Preparedness

Anyone who has worked in a large office or factory will be familiar with fire and earthquake drills and other emergency procedures. Large communities and particularly those consisting of mid and higher rise buildings will have equivalent processes and procedures. When an emergency occurs, there will be an announcement identifying the type of emergency and location. In addition to fire and earthquake alerts, there may be other alerts for intruders and lost health/memory-care residents.

A community will solicit able-bodied residents to act as building and floor captains, whose function is to ensure that residents promptly exit a danger zone or shelter in a protected location. Drills will periodically occur.

Summary

You have learned that settling-in and adjusting to a Life Plan Community is more complicated and time-consuming than moving into a house or apartment. In addition to arranging your living unit, you've been introduced to communal living with protocols, rules and routines; like what a college student experiences when entering in a fraternity or sorority. The difference is you'll have control of the extent of your involvement in the myriad of programs and activities offered.

Chapter 16

Role of Family and Heirs

Most residents entering independent living are physically and mentally able to take care of themselves and had the initiative and wherewithal to evaluate, select, and successfully move in on their own. Others may have had their children or siblings initiate their interest and assist them in the selection of a community and with the process of moving in. All family members should be supportive while new residents adjust to their new living arrangements and assimilate into the community.

As they age, a resident's capacity will likely diminish. How steep the decline is will vary greatly among residents? However, many will need assistance at some point. And of these, most will recognize their need and take the initiative to arrange for their care within the community. But there will be a few in denial or unaware of their condition who become a risk to themselves or others. This is when the family should get involved.

Family Oversight

Most life plan community residents have at least one close family member within a day's drive who periodically visits them. With the marvels of smartphones, Facebook, and other social media, remote family members should be regularly in touch and aware of any troubling conditions. If they sense a problem, they need to contact the community's resident services manager and ask for an assessment.

Conversely, a community's staff holds periodic meetings to review comments and observations from staff members and residents regarding individuals who are not managing well or are out of control. When a community senses a need to intervene and cannot convince the resident to accept help, the resident services manager contacts the family member(s) having durable power of attorney for finances and personal and   care and perhaps other family members who are close by or frequent visitors for a conference on the resident's condition and how to proceed.

The family's role is as an advocate for the resident, and they may enlist the assistance of a professional in these matters. Their task is to work with the resident and management to arrive at a suitable course of action. Health-care advocates may be found at the National Association of Health Advocacy Consultants (NAHAC). Also, consider contacting gerontology case managers, who can be found in appendix B, Resources.

If the resident moves into the health center and vacates the independent living unit, the family may have to assume responsibility for transferring furnishings and personal items to the resident's new living quarters and clearing out the remaining furnishings and possessions so the unit can be available for a new resident.

At the passing of a resident, the family governs notification to the community. Should the surviving spouse or family have a public memorial, the time and place of that memorial will also be posted. Generally, the service will be off-site, and the family can expect significant attendance if the resident was active and popular in the community.

Heirs

The role of an executor and heirs of a deceased resident varies depending on the type of contract the resident had with the community.

Contracts with Reimbursements

The specific obligations will be stated in the resident's agreement at move-in. Be sure to have read the contract. The contract will have a refundable entrance fee, so the executor's goal is to quickly vacate the living unit and satisfy any open obligations, such as damage exceeding normal wear and tear. If the resident had made tenant improvements, management may require compensation to return the unit to its original condition. It will depend on their assessment as to what a new resident would likely prefer and the relative cost of maintenance.

Fee-for-Service Contracts

Again, the specific obligations will be stated in the resident's agreement at move-in. It is likely that the monthly fee continues until the living unit is vacated. There should not be a charge for normal wear and tear, and there could be a damage deposit, which may be partially or fully refundable.

Vacating the Living Unit

Clearing out a living unit can be a daunting task, particularly if it is brimming with possessions helter-skelter. Try completing one room at a time rather than moving back and forth. The community's maintenance staff may be available to assist in disassembly and removal of large items on a time and material basis.

If the community has a secondhand store, they may accept usable furnishings, kitchenware, clothing, and personal items. Contact them before you begin because they may agree to clear out everything left in place after the family takes what they want. Management, on the other hand, may charge for removal of what is left

Summary

This chapter is for the family and heirs. Residents should review it and store a copy with their will.

While life plan communities provide residents with wellness, social and recreational programs as well as a continuum of health care, their family needs to be aware of what is happening and intervene as necessary. Family members need to be observant, good listeners, and an advocate for the resident. If a resident is incapable of making a good decision, the family needs to step up and play the parent role.

Appendixes

Appendices

Mortality and Senior Illnesses

I purposely left this for last because it is scary without considering all the support systems described in this book.

Mortality

From the Iron Age up until the Industrial Revolution, life expectancy was approximately thirty-five years. However, this number was an average and skewed by a very high infant and youth mortality rate. Those who reached adulthood could most likely expect to live into their mid- to late-forties. By 1900, improved nutrition, better sanitation, and contributions from bacteriologists increased life expectancy at birth to 47.3 years. The period between 1900 and 1950 added twenty years in longevity from birth due to the widespread usage of antibiotics and much improved standards in cleanliness, hygiene, and sanitation. Life expectancy by then was 68.2 years.[53]

Figure A.1 illustrates an increase in life expectancy that averages approximately one year per decade over the last several decades. The difference between male and female life expectancy ballooned to 4.2 years in 1980, but has since retracted to 2.7 years.

---

[53] Our World in Data, "Life Expectancy, 1543 to 2011," Max Roser, https://ourworldindata.org/life-expectancy/ .

Seniors are Living Longer

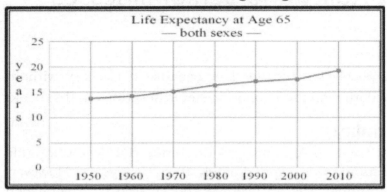

Figure A.1. Change in Life Expectancy 54

How long you may expect to live

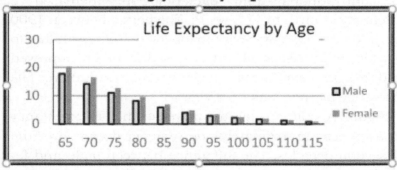

Figure A.2. Life Expectancy by Age [55]

---

54 "Table 22, Life Expectancy at Birth" National Center for Health Statistics, CDC/NCHS, 2011 https://www.cdc.gov/nchs/data/hus/2011/022.pdf .
55 "Actuarial Table", Social Security Administration, 2014, https://www.ssa.gov/oact/STATS/table4c6.html .

Common Disabling Illnesses of the Elderly

Seniors face a variety of ailments and disease that they most likely did not experience during their earlier years. Common and chronic illnesses may be more frequent and harder to fend off. Following are illnesses and hazards that many seniors experience.

As Seniors Age

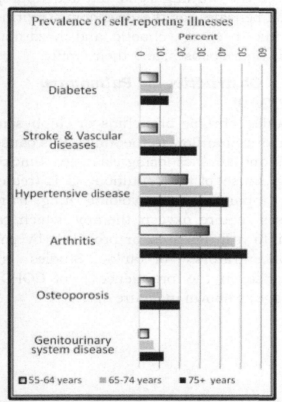

Figure A.3 Disabling illnesses of the elderly [56]

---

[56] Source: Australian Institute of Health & Welfare (AIHW), 2015

252 | APPENDIX A

As people age they are likely to reach the point where continuing to live independently in their homes becomes a struggle , if not dangerous or impossible . Usually there is a gradual awakening with time to react since many illnesses develop slowly.

Elderly illnesses are generally out of sight and out of mind until people reach their sixties . If one does not heed the warning signs and take appropriate steps to compensate for the developing infirmities , their lives may become chaotic and hazardous for themselves, their spouses, and their family.

Chronic Obstructive Pulmonary Disease (COPD)

COPD includes chronic bronchitis or emphysema . It results in reduced airflow to the lungs. It is caused by the airways and air sacs losing elasticity. Smoking is the leading cause of the condition . It is treated by medicated inhalers and avoiding lung irritants . Severe cases require oxygen therapy , which can be plumbed into a living area or provided by portable oxygen concentrators or tanks . Studies show a stepwise rise in the prevalence of COPD with advancing age as shown in Figure A.4.

Has Breathing Becoming a Problem?

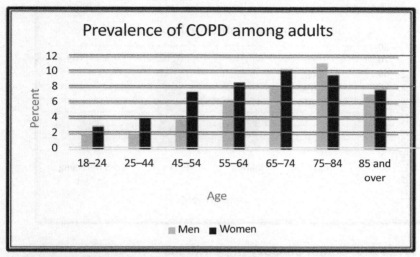

Figure A.4. COPD prevalence in the United States 57

Sensory Problems

Our quality of life is dependent on our senses. We need good vision for working, reading, attending plays and movies, and enjoying sports and a sunset, to name only a few. Hearing is essential to music, social interaction, and warning of danger. Feeling is needed for work, play , and awareness of our surroundings . Good balance is dependent upon your inner ear, which controls your positioning, and feeling in your feet. As you age, these sensory attributes may diminish or become compromised as shown in Figure A.5.

---

57 CDC/NCHS Data Brief, Number 63, Fig. 2, 2007–2009, https://www.cdc.gov/nchs/data/databriefs/db63.pdf .

Frailty begins in the seventies

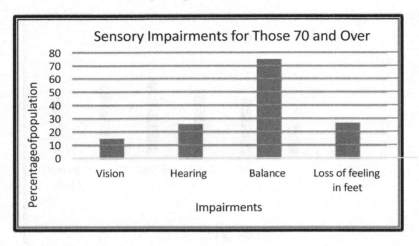

Figure A.5. Senior sensory impairments ⁵⁸

Vision

The four most common elderly vision problems are cataracts , diabetic issues , glaucoma , and macular degeneration, in the order as shown in Figure A.6.

It is not surprising that cataracts are the leading incidence of eye problems among seniors . Yet surgical treatment for cataracts is highly successful , modestly priced , and covered by Medicare and most insurance policies . Even the botched cataract surgery that I had was rectified with two follow-up surgeries, providing 20/ 20 vision.

⁵⁸ "Vision, Hearing, Balance and Sensory Impairment in Americans Aged 70 and Over: United States, 1999-2006C", NCHS Data Brief No. 31, April 2010

https://www.cdc.gov/nchs/data/databriefs/db31.pdf .

Will, I lose my driving privileges?

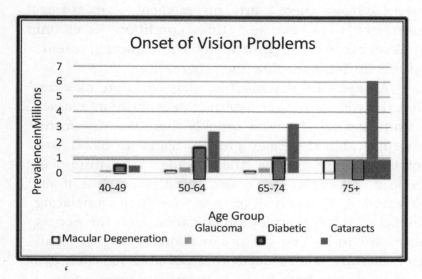

Figure A.6. Common vision problems of the elderly.[59]

The second most common eye problem is diabetic retinopathy, a complication of diabetes. Retinopathy happens when high blood sugar damages the tiny blood vessels of the retina. The condition will worsen over time. If blood sugar remains high; it will lead to poor vision and even blindness. Those who can control their diabetes should be able to mitigate the problem.

Macular Degeneration

Macular Degeneration causes loss of central vision. There are two types, "dry" and "wet." Almost 85 to 90 percent of those with macular degeneration have the dry form, which damages the retina. The progression of dry macular degeneration is slow, and it may take years for

---

[59] Prevent Blindness America, 2012.

it to worsen . Often one eye is affected more than the other . While there are no medical or surgical treatments to reverse this condition , vitamin supplements with high doses of antioxidants , lutein, and zeaxanthin may slow the progression.

An eye with dry macular degeneration may develop the wet kind. Wet macular degeneration causes vi- sion loss much more quickly than the dry form. Abnormal blood -vessel growth leads to blood and protein leakage below the macula . The unnoticed bleeding will eventually cause rapid vision loss if left untreated. A re- cently developed treatment, consisting of periodic injec- tions of a medication into the eye, is successful in halting the progression of the wet form. Laser therapy is also used . It is possible for each eye to have either or both forms of macular degeneration.

Glaucoma

Unlike macular degeneration , glaucoma reduces periph - eral vision and greatly extends the time for eyes to adjust when going from a light to a dark environment . Glau- coma is often referred to as the " silent thief of sight ." Once lost , vision cannot be recovered, so treatment is aimed at preventing further loss . Approximately 10 per- cent of those over eighty have glaucoma. Elevated intra- ocular pressure is the main reason for developing glaucoma.

Eye drops that lower the eye pressure are the most common treatment for preventing the progression . Laser iridotomy , trabeculectomy , and a drainage implant can slow the progression as well . Glaucoma may occur as early as age fifty , and symptoms may not appear until the disease is well advanced. Left untreated, it can lead to permanent damage and progress to blindness.

Family history is a risk factor for both glaucoma and macular degeneration. In addition to diminishing one's quality of life, it is dangerous to drive a car with impaired vision from either macular degeneration or glaucoma. Seniors experiencing the onset of these conditions need to plan for the eventual loss of driving privileges if treatment does not abate the illness.

Hearing

Most hearing loss is due to persistent or extreme noise exposure. Many seniors currently in their eighties and nineties suffered war or occupational hearing loss. Fortunately, OSHA began regulating occupational noise exposure in the 1970s. Persistent loud music at concerts and other entertainment venues can also contribute to hearing loss. Heredity and certain medical conditions can contribute to hearing loss. There is also age-related hearing loss, which occurs gradually with age. About a third of people over age sixty-five have some age-related hearing loss.

While there is no known single cause for age-related hearing loss, it is commonly caused as tiny hairs inside the inner ear become damaged or die. The hair cells do not regrow, so hearing loss is permanent.

While some hearing loss can be treated with medication and surgery, age-related hearing loss is not curable and can only be helped with hearing aids and assistive listening devices, which pick up the sound

close to the source and transmit it wirelessly to the recipient's hearing aid or portable receiver.

Please speak up.

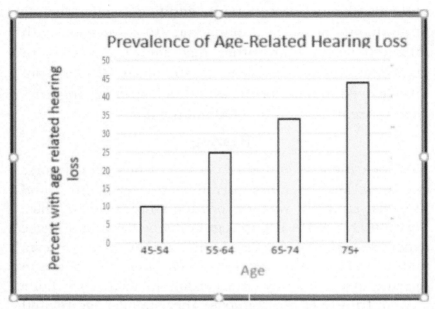

Figure A.7. Prevalence of age-related hearing loss

60 *Falling Risks*

Falls are the leading cause of injury-related visits to
emergency rooms in the United States and the primary
cause of accidental deaths in people over the age of sixty
- five years. Figure A.8 illustrates that seniors are twice
as likely to be hospitalized as their younger brethren,
and their stay in a hospital will be approximately a day
longer. The data relate to physical ailments and do not
include mental disabilities.

---

60 Blevins et al., 2015; National Institute of Deafness & other Communication Disorders (NIDCD), 2016.

Here Again!

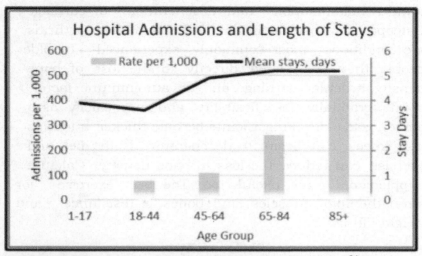

Figure A.8. Hospital admissions in the United States [61]

Poor balance, skeletal problems, and neuropathy contribute to the disproportionate share of falls among seniors. More than 90 percent of hip fractures occur because of falls, with most of these fractures occurring in people over seventy years of age.

Balance

The inner ear signals the body's vestibular and skeletal systems to maintain balance. If these systems do not respond rapidly, a fall is likely and often results in broken limbs or head injuries.

Skeletal Problems

The most significant effect of aging on the skeletal system is the progressive reduction in bone density that occurs in

---

[61] Healthcare Cost and Utilization Project (HCUP), 2012.

both sexes from about the age of fifty and a tendency toward inflammation and degeneration of cartilage . Osteoporosis , osteoarthritis , and rheumatoid arthritis are conditions most commonly experienced by older people ; they are related directly to the loss of bone density, articular cartilage, and an autoimmune factor. Joints gradually lose flexibility and may calcify as a person gets older. Finger joints become thicker, and hips and knees can begin to degenerate . Both diet and exercise can reduce the loss in bone density . Calcium supplements are useful too . The best exercise for strengthening muscles and bones is resistance and weight lifting.

Neuropathy

Some elders suffer from neuropathy that damages the peripheral nervous system . It is especially evident in people over fifty-five and affects approximately 4 percent of that population . Neuropathy usually causes pain and numbness in the hands and feet. The most common cause of neuropathy is diabetes . It can also result from traumatic injuries , infections , metabolic disorders , and exposure to toxins. It lowers the quality of life and raises the risk of falling.

Elders with nerve damage in the feet should not drive a motor vehicle. All too often one reads about an elderly person driving into a storefront because he or she could not stop. Rarely is it a problem with the car.

Autoimmune Disease

Age-related changes in the immune system lead to decreased immune function and increased vulnerability to infectious diseases and cancer in older people . As people age , their autoimmune system declines in its effectiveness due in large part to oxidative damage caused by the recurrent presence of significant amounts of free radicals. (Free radicals are highly reactive, unstable molecules that readily damage proteins, lipids, and other cellular components.) In aging, the decreased production of antioxidant enzymes causes a buildup of damaged proteins and other molecules that can be toxic to cells.

To illustrate the problem, 90 percent of young adults respond to most vaccines. However, for elderly individuals the effectiveness of vaccines against influenza-like illness is 23 percent.[62] About 90 percent of influenza deaths occur in people over age sixty-five.

There are several nutritional steps for strengthening the immune system, such as eating cold-water fish for their Omega-3 fatty acids, taking L-glutathione and spirulina for their antioxidants, and ingesting vitamins E, B6, and C.

Strokes

Nearly three-fourths of all strokes occur in people over the age of sixty-five. The risk of having a stroke more than doubles each decade after the age of fifty-five. A transient ischemic attack (*TIA*), that happens when blood flow to part of the brain is blocked or reduce, is often a precursor to a stroke. However, strokes can occur without warning and time for preparation.

The effects of a stroke differ for everyone. It is dependent on the part of the brain injured, how bad the event is, and the person's general health. Strokes may

---

[62] *The Lancet*, "Efficacy and Effectiveness of Influenza Vaccines in Elderly People," September 22, 2005.

result in weakness , paralysis , numbness , problems with balance , memory , or thinking , tiredness , and problems with bladder or bowel control. A stroke can be devastat - ing to the spouse and family as well as the patient.

Recovering stroke patients may require modification to their living space to accommodate their loss of mobility. Changes may be temporary or permanent, depending on the patient's degree of recovery . Access to a support group for the caregiver is important.

Mental Decline

Mental decline is perhaps seniors ' greatest fear in growing old. Everyone is aware of ancestors , neighbors , or friends exhibiting some degree of mental decline. It comes in various forms and intensities . Depending on the cause , good nutrition and mental and physical exercise may forestall the onset of some conditions . However, there are few available cures. Treatments are mostly limited to providing a soothing and familiar environment and assistance with activities of daily living as needed.

Age-related Cognitive Decline

As people age, they usually have mild memory impairment and process information more slowly . Their brains frequently decrease in volume, and some nerve cells, or neurons , are lost. These changes , called age-related cog - nitive decline , are normal and are not considered as signs of dementia.

Mild Cognitive Impairment

Some people develop cognitive and memory problems that are not severe enough to be diagnosed as dementia, but are more pronounced than the cognitive changes associated with normal aging. Generally, their condition does not interfere with everyday activities. Many may later develop dementia.

Dementia

Dementia develops when the parts of the brain that are involved with learning, memory, decision making, and language are affected by one or more of a variety of infections or diseases. Dementia usually first appears as forgetfulness. It is important to determine the type of dementia because 20 percent of cases are treatable.

Types of dementia are the following:

+ **Lewy body disease**, a leading cause of dementia in elderly adults. People with this condition have abnormal protein structures in certain areas of the brain.

+ **Vascular dementia,** caused by many small strokes.

+ **Illnesses** that may lead to dementia include multiple sclerosis, Parkinson's disease, Lyme disease, and progressive supra-nuclear-palsy.

Alzheimer's Disease

Alzheimer's is in class of its own by accounting for 50 percent or more of all dementia. About one in eight older Americans is afflicted with this disease. About half of people over eighty years of age will develop Alzheimer's disease. It is a progressive decline in cognitive function over a period of several years that erodes memory and reduces the ability to perform tasks. It goes through three stages, each with a definite set of symptoms that define the stage.

Mild Alzheimer 's. The first sign of early or mild Alzheimer 's disease is some memory loss. People with mild Alzheimer's often forget where they put their car keys or are unable to remember the names of people and objects, and may substitute a word for the one they 've forgotten. Forgetfulness occurs with regularity. Short-term memory loss will be very evident.

As the disease progresses, the symptoms may become more noticeable to family and friends. People with mild Alzheimer's may repeat questions, get lost in once-familiar areas, and have trouble remembering what they've just read or heard. It may be difficult, if not im-possible, for them to learn new things. As they become more forgetful, they will often get quieter, withdraw from social situations, and become moody.

Moderate Alzheimer 's. People with moderate Alzheimer 's may begin to have trouble recognizing their family members and friends. They may forget what day of the week it is or simple details about their past. They may have difficulty getting dressed and performing tasks they once did with ease. Eventually simple tasks like eat-ing or going to the bathroom will be a challenge. They may begin to sleep more during the day than at night.

Personality changes may cause hallucinations, delusions, paranoia, or compulsive behavior. They may become angry and even violent, hitting, kicking, or screaming out of frustration.

Severe Alzheimer 's. People with severe Alzheimer 's are unable to respond to the people around them. They lose the ability to walk, talk, and care for themselves. They must rely on caregivers to handle even their most basic needs, including eating, washing, and assistance in the bathroom.

People at the end of this Alzheimer's stage can no longer sit unsupported or hold up their heads. They have trouble eating or refuse to eat because swallowing is difficult. They are unable to control their urination or bowel movements.

Alzheimer's disease progresses differently for each person. Some may live for ten years and others as long as twenty years. Death is usually caused by complications, such as an infection or fall, rather than Alzheimer's.

Caring for Alzheimer's Patients

Early-onset. Alzheimer's patients can function well if they follow a familiar routine. They can carry on a conversation if it is on routine subjects or on their personal historic events. As the disease progresses, their care and supervision needs will increase until they require full-time assistance.

Mild stage. People in the mild stage can live independently in the care of a family member who can assist with some of the activities of daily living (ADL), such as assisting in bathing and dressing. The caregiver will need to reduce the patient's choices to a few to eliminate frustration. As an example, reduce wardrobe choices to a couple rather than many. Be patient and eliminate distractions.

Later stages. As an Alzheimer's patient progresses be-yond the mild stage, the spouse or family should con-sider long-term care options, such as respite care, assisted living, memory care (assisted living with special emphasis on Alzheimer 's needs), and in extreme cases, skilled nursing. Caring for an Alzheimer 's patient beyond the mild stage is a 24-7 endeavor and will overwhelm a single care provider. It cannot be done without assis-tance.

Summary

Aging is not for sissies . Seniors need to be aware of health changes, social isolation and physical hazards. They need to participate in wellness activities and plan for future care if needed.

Resources

Frederick's Website. http://agingsmartly.org

Features interactive mapping of over sixteen hundred Life Plan Communities and providing access to their websites. Also provides trends, current community development and resident experiences.

Associations

✦ Aging Life Care Association, (ALCA), Formerly National Association of Professional Geriatric Care Managers, http://www.aginglifecare.org/ and http://memberfinder.caremanager.org/index.php/ff/advancedSearch#results

✦ CARF International Accreditation, http://carf.org/Accreditation/AccreditationProcess/

✦ Commission for Case Manager Certification, https://ccmcertification.org

✦ LeadingAge, an association for nonprofit health-care providers, http://www.leadingage.org/

✦ Life Plan Community Organization, http://lifeplancommunity.org/

✦ National Academy of Certified Care Managers, http://www.naccm.net/

✦ National Association of Social Workers (NASW), http://www.naswdc.org/

- National Center for Assisted Living (NCAL), https://www.ahcancal.org/ncal/Pages/index.aspx
- State Regulations, posted by NCAL, https://www.ahcancal.org/ncal/advocacy/regs/Pages/AssistedLivingRegulations.aspx
- National Continuing Care Residents Association, (NaCCRA), www.naccra.com/

US Government Agencies

- Agency for Health-care Research and Quality, HCUPnet, http://hcupnet.ahrq.gov/
- Social Security Administration, Life Expectancy-Actuarial Table, 2013, https://www.ssa.gov/oact/STATS/table4c6.html
- U.S. Securities and Exchange Commission EDGAR Company Filings. https://www.sec.gov/edgar/searchedgar/companysearch.html
- Government Accounting Office, "Report to Special Committee on Aging, US Senate," June 2010, http://www.gao.gov/new.items/d10611.pdf
- Centers for Disease Control and Prevention (CDC), National Center for Health Statistics https://www.cdc.gov/nchs/
- Centers for Medicare & Medicaid Services, http://cms.gov

+ CMS database at data.medicare.gov, https://data.medicare.gov. Also see https://data.medicare.gov/data/archives/nursing-home-compare.

+ CMS Five Star Rating System Detail, https://www.cms.gov/medicare/provider-enrollment-and-certification/certificationandcomplianc/fsqrs.html

+ CDC/NCHS Data Brief on COPD prevalence in the United States, Number 63, Fig. 2, 2007–2009 https://www.cdc.gov/nchs/data/databriefs/db63.pdf

+ Health-care Cost and Utilization Project (HCUP-US),. User Support, https://www.hcup-us.ahrq.gov/

+ National Institute of Deafness and other Communication Disorders (NIDCD), https://www.nidcd.nih.gov/health/age-related-hearing-loss

+ National Center for Health Statistics (NCHS), https://www.cdc.gov/nchs/

Community Groups

+ Oregon Senior Referral Agency Association OSRAA), http://osraa.com/

+ Village to Village Network, http://vtvnetwork.org

Others

+ Australian Institute of Health and Welfare, Disabling illnesses of the elderly. 2014, Fig. 6.27

http://www.aihw.gov.au/WorkArea/DownloadAsset.aspx?id=60129547764

✦ Case-Shiller home price indices, absolute and inflation adjusted, 2000–2016, https://en.wikipedia.org/wiki/Case%E2%80%93Shiller_index#/media/File:Case_shiller_janv09.jpg

✦ Cattell's personality factors can be found at http://psychology.about.com/od/trait-theories-personality/a/16-personality-factors.htm and http://en.wikipedia.org/wiki/16_Personality_Factors

✦ GuideStar, http://guidestar.org

✦ Fixr, Inc., Disability Modeling Cost, May 2017, https://www.fixr.com/costGuides.html#group_b07be56f0d7282ab73b04ebc7f4a48e0

✦ MeMetLife, The Maturing of America—Communities Moving Forward for an Aging Population, 2011 https://www.metlife.com/assets/cao/foundation/MaturingOfAmerica_FINAL_Rpt.pdf

✦ Prevent Blindness America, vision problems in the United States, http://www.visionproblemsus.org/.

✦ Prince Market Research, "Clarity Final Report: Aging in America", August 20, 2007, https://www.slideshare.net/clarityproducts/clarity-2007-aginig-in-place-in-america-2836029

✦

Index

About the Author

Writing a book on a retirement facility is subjective as well as factual. My slant on the information that I convey here is influenced by my personal experience. My wife and I live as independent residents in Mirabella- Seattle, a life plan community. We have been active in the resident association and its committees. We have previously held offices on a condominium board.

In selecting a life plan community as our final home, we were greatly influenced by our experience of being care providers for our elderly parents and a cousin with Alzheimer's disease. My parents were active and appeared to be healthy into their mid-eighties. Then calamity struck, with my father suffering a stroke, followed by discovering that my mother had dementia that my father had successfully covered up. This started a lengthy progression of moves for my parents, beginning with light assisted living and ending in skilled nursing care. I tried to convince them to move into a community, but my mother was overwhelmed by its immensity and refused. My mother was in five different care facilities prior to her death at age ninety-five.

From our experience in caring for our parents and a cousin, the offering of a continuum of care facility was very appealing. Further, we wished to make our own choice and not burden our children.

The abundance of social and wellness activities along with the opportunity to enter a new community influenced our entry at a younger age than most community residents.

Made in the USA
Las Vegas, NV
15 November 2023

80876867R00167